A Road To The Expert Title

IM Eric Tangborn

CHESS DIGEST, INC

ISBN: 0-87568-270-7

Computer use courtesy of *Inside Chess*. For a complete catalogue of *International Chess Enterprise* books and chess accessories, or for a subscription to *Inside Chess*, published through *I.C.E.* U.S. P.O. Box 19457, Seattle, WA 98109, USA. 1-800-26-CHESS, Fax: (206) 441-4736

Author: Eric Tangborn
Editor: Ken Smith
Computer Typesetting: Eric Tangborn
Cover: Elaine Smith
Final Proof: Sid Pickard
Final Preparation: Eric Tangborn
Diagrams: Jonathan Berry's *YesWeDoDiagrams* Program

Publisher: Chess Digest, Inc.® 1601 Tantor (P.O. Box 59029) Dallas, Texas 75229

Introduction

The aim of this book is to focus on just what is necessary to become an expert. The important topics can be divided into three categories:

1) You need an opening repertoire which fits your style and in which you have great confidence. Preferably the opening should be simple and not require a great deal of memorization. The way to learn an opening is by studying complete games and learning the strategies and tactics of typical positions. Former World Champion Tigran Petrosian has written that the best and perhaps the only way to chess mastery is by studying games played by masters.

2) You need to have good positional judgement. That is, you need to have a strong feel for where to put your pieces and how to take advantage of structural weaknesses.

3) You must be very sharp tactically. The best way to improve is to practice finding combinations. Buy a book on combinations and when you have a few spare moments, try to solve a few positions.

This book gives you a complete opening repetoire as well as tips on improving your strategical and tactical abilities.

In addition to studying the lessons in this book, you should do the following:

1) Good prerequisites to this book are: *Play Winning Chess, Winning Chess Tactics*, and *Winning Chess Strategies* by Yasser Seirawan with Jeremy Silman. A subscription to *Inside Chess* is also recommended (see page 2).

2) Study well-annotated games played by masters.

3) Play competitively on a regular basis. Just as important, annotate your games and try to learn from your mistakes.

Table of Contents

An Opening for White: The King's Indian Attack

The opening in chess refers to that phase of the game during which the forces of both sides are mobilized to encounter each other in the middlegame. At the start of the game one should be striving for these four elements in the opening: 1) the fight for control of the center; 2) the striving for the quickest and most active development; 3) the creation of conditions that permit early castling; 4) the formation of an advantageous pawn structure.

The King's Indian Attack is a simple opening that satisfies these elements. The opening moves for White are: 1.Nf3, 2.g3, 3.Bg2, 4.O-O, 5.d3.

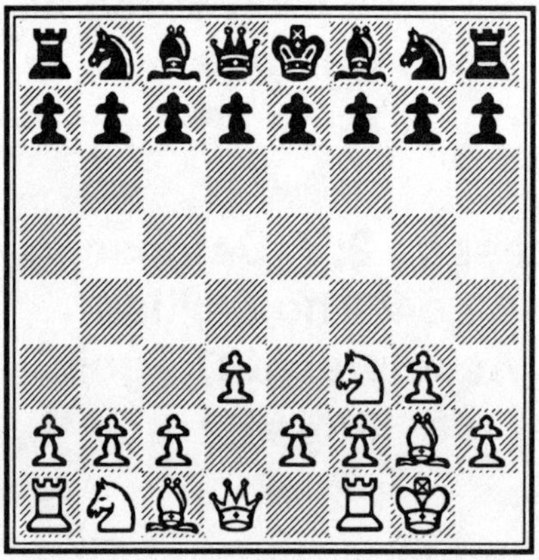

The first plan will be to advance the pawn to e4, if necessary preceded by moves such as Nbd2 and Re1.

The next plans will depend on what Black has played in the meantime. Usually White attacks on the kingside, but he can also concentrate on the queenside. This chapter will be devoted to such ideas.

Part 1

1.Nf3 c5 2.g3 Nc6 3.Bg2 g6 4.O-O Bg7 5.d3

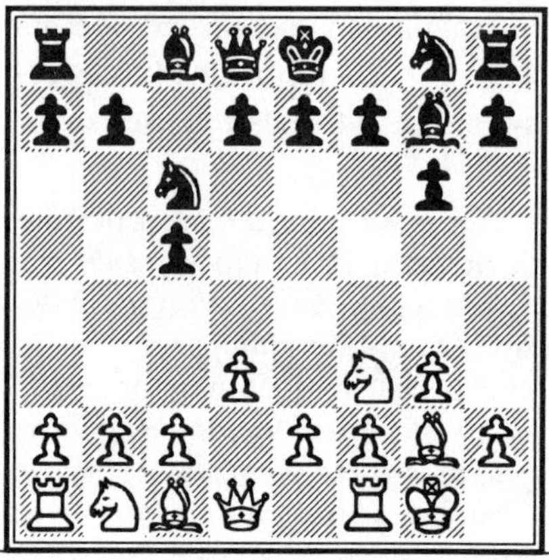

Illustrative Game 1

GM Tigran Petrosian
NM Max Pavey

Moscow 1955

1.e4 c5 2.Nf3 d6 3.d3

In many games the King's Indian Attack is reached by transposition.

3...Nc6 4.Nbd2 Nf6 5.g3 e6

Too passive. Better is 5...g6.

6.Bg2 Be7 7.O-O O-O 8.c3 d5

Black fights for control of the center, but loses a tempo moving his d-pawn twice.

9.Re1 Qc7

Not a good square for the Queen, as it will be hassled by White's QB. Better is 9...b5.

10.Nf1 Bd7

This square should be reserved for the Knight.

11.e5

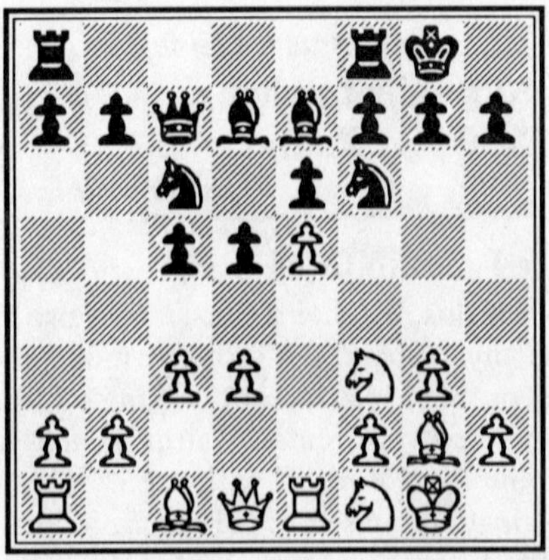

This is the key move in this type of position (when Black places his pawns on d5 and e6). The pawn on e5 has a cramping influence on Black's position and usually when he allows it he will be at a disadvantage. It cuts Black's position in half and makes it difficult to maneuver the pieces between the queenside and kingside. White's following maneuvers are very characteristic and will be seen in many games in this book.

11...Ne8

The Knight would have been better placed at d7. This is why Black's tenth move was a mistake. Black should try to start counterplay on the queenside (beginning with ...b5) but his pieces are misplaced and he will be slowed down.

12.Bf4

Prevents the freeing maneuver ...f6 or ...f5.

12...Qb6 13.Qe2 Bd8 14.h4

A very important move. White's plan is to play h5 and h6, creating a big weakness at f6. This move is also played to enable a piece to be placed on g5, where it threatens the Black King, and to use the h2-square as a transfer point for the Knight.

14...Qa6 15.h5 Ne7 16.h6 g6 17.Bg5 Rc8 18.N1h2

Another very important move. The Knight heads to g4 where it eyes the weakness at f6.

18...Bb5 19.Bf1 Nf5 20.Ng4 Qb6 21.Qd2 Bc6

Black has been aimlessly maneuvering his pieces without a coherent plan.

22.Bxd8 Qxd8 23.d4 Qe7 24.Bd3 Kh8 25.Kg2

White slowly improves the position of his pieces. He can take his time as Black has no counterplay. The idea behind the last move is to be able to move the Rook to the h-file if it is needed there.

25...Rc7 26.b4

Opening the c-file would be to White's advantage. Hence Black closes the queenside, but this allows White to concentrate his forces on the kingside.

26...c4 27.Bc2 Qd8 28.Qg5

White decides that the endgame is the easiest way to decisively increase his advantage. If Black tries to avoid the exchange of Queens with 28...Qc8, then 29.Nf6 would allow the Queen to penetrate to the g7 square.

28...Qxg5 29.Nxg5 Ne7

Moving the Knight on f5 to a more passive position only worsens Black's position.

30.Re3

White continues to improve the position of his pieces. The Rook moves to f3, where it pressures the weakness at f7.

30...Ng8 31.Rf3 Re7

Perhaps Black felt that his position could not be cracked, but now comes the decisive combination.

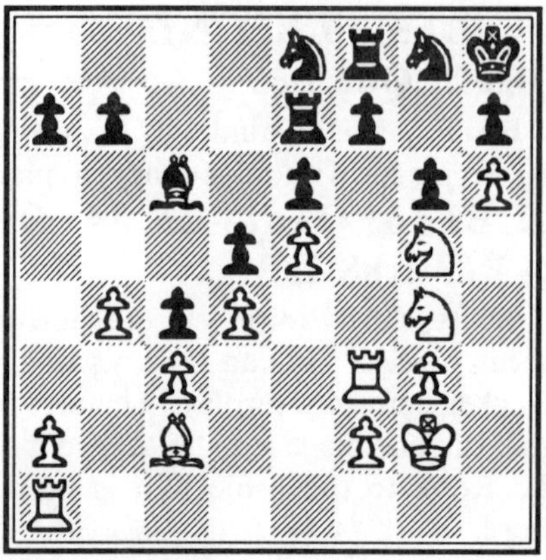

32.Bxg6! hxg6 33.h7

Black loses his Knight on g8. The position is opened and Black is not able to defend against the invading pieces. White plans to play Rh1, hxg8(Q)+, Nf6+, exf6, g4, and Rfh3, mating on the h-file.

33...f5 34.Rh1

The f-pawn is pinned. White now plans Rf4, hxg8(Q)+, Nh6+, Rfh4 threatening Nxf5+ and again mating with his Rooks on the h-file.

34...Ngf6 35.Nxf6 Nxf6 36.exf6 Rxf6 37.Re3

White is easily winning. The passed pawn on h7 and weakness at e6 completely tie down Black's pieces. It is the weakness at g6 that will provide the final breakthrough.

37...Re8 38.Rh4 Bd7 39.Kf3

The King is not to be left out of the action. It will take up a commanding post at e5, where it threatens further penetration.

39...Kg7 40.Kf4 Bc8 41.Re1 Rff8 42.Ke5 Rh8 43.Reh1 Re7

If 43...Rhf8, the exchange of Rooks after 44.h8(Q)+ wins easily for White.

44.a4 Ree8 45.a5 Rd8 46.Rh6 Rde8 47.Nf3 Re7 48.Nh4 1-0

Either 48...Kxh6 49.Nxf5+ or the g6 square falls.

Illustrative Game 2

GM Bobby Fischer
GM Oscar Panno

Buenos Aires 1970

1.e4 c5 2.Nf3 e6 3.d3

Of this, Fischer writes: "This used to be my favorite. I thought it led to a favorable variation of the King's Indian reversed, particularly after Black has committed himself with ...e6." (*My 60 Memorable Games*: Simon & Schuster 1969).

3...Nc6 4.g3 g6 5.Bg2 Bg7 6.O-O Nge7 7.Re1 d6 8.c3 O-O 9.d4 cxd4

Better was 9...b6 to keep the center from being closed.

10.cxd4 d5 11.e5

Now White will be able to attack on the kingside without worrying about counterplay in the center.

11...Bd7 12.Nc3 Rc8 13.Bf4 Na5

Possibly 13...f6 should be played to blunt White's coming kingside attack.

14.Rc1 b5 15.b3!

A good defensive move that slows Black on the queenside. Black's pieces are not in good position to take advantage of the resulting weaknesses at c3 and a3.

15...b4 16.Ne2 Bb5 17.Qd2 Nac6 18.g4

White starts moving his pieces toward the kingside. With his last move White creates a square for the Knight on g3. 18...Bxe2 should now be played, although this would give up important squares that the Bishop controls.

18...a5? 19.Ng3 Qb6 20.h4 Nb8

Black will maneuver this Knight to f8 for defensive purposes.

21.Bh6

Exchanging Black's most important

defensive piece and creating dark square weaknesses at f6 and h6. Nh5 becomes a possible threat.

21...Nd7 22.Qg5 Rxc1 23.Rxc1 Bxh6 24.Qxh6 Rc8 25.Rxc8+ Nxc8 26.h5

The loosening of the g6 square will later play a decisive role.

26...Qd8?

Now White will be able to finish the game with a very beautiful combination. Better is 26...Nf8. White would still have a very big advantage. One plan is to play 27.Qf4 followed by h6 and Ng5. Black will be forced to play ...Qe7 after which White can seize the c-file with Qc1. He could then start a pawn storm with f4-f5.

27.Ng5 Nf8

28.Be4!

A very elegant move which at first looks like a typo. White intentionally places a piece en prise, as Black will be checkmated if he captures the Bishop: 28...dxe4 29.N3xe4 followed by 30.Nf6+. Thus the Bishop will play a decisive role on the b1-h7 diagonal.

28...Qe7

Perhaps the best defense is 28...Be8, protecting the vulnerable pawns on f7 and g6. If White retreats the Bishop with 29.Bb1, Black gets counterplay after 29...Qc7. Instead, Fischer probably intended 29.hxg6 hxg6 (29...fxg6? 30.Qxf8+) 30.Nh5 gxh5 31.Nh7 (31.Bh7+ Nxh7 32.Nxh7 f6 is unclear) 31...Nxh7 32.Bxh7+ Kh8 33.Bd3+ Kg8 34.Qh7+ Kf8 35.Qh8+ Ke7 36.Qf6+ Kd7 37.gxh5 and White wins because the h-pawn is unstoppable. For example, 37...Qb6 38.h6 Qxd4 39.Bb5+ or 37...Ne7 38.h6 Ng8 39.Qxd8+ Kxd8 40.h7.

29.Nxh7! Nxh7 30.hxg6 fxg6

Question 1: What does White play against 30...Nf8.

31.Bxg6

Threatening both 32.Bxh7+ Qxh7 33.Qxe6+ and 32.Nh5.

31...Ng5

Or 31...Qg7 32.Bxh7+ Kh8 33.Qxg7+ Kxg7 34.Bb1 Ne7 35.f4 Nf6 36.Kf2 with an easily won endgame.

32.Nh5 Nf3+ 33.Kg2 Nh4+ 34.Kg3 Nxg6 35.Nf6+ Kf7 36.Qh7+ 1-0

36...Kf8 37.Qg8 mate.

Illustrative Game 3

GM Tigran Petrosian
GM Ludek Pachman

Bled 1961

1.Nf3 c5 2.g3 Nc6 3.Bg2 g6 4.O-O Bg7 5.d3 e6 6.e4 Nge7 7.Re1 O-O

7...d6 should have been played to prevent White's next move.

8.e5 d6

Perhaps a better idea is 8...Qc7 9.Qe2 b6 and 10...Bb7. Now Black's c-pawn is weak and White will have the c4 outpost for his Knight and f4 for his Bishop.

9.exd6 Qxd6 10.Nbd2

Threatening 10.Ne4. Now Black should not try 10...Nd4 11.Ne4 Qc7 12.Bf4 e5 13.Nxe5 Bxe5 14.Nf6+ winning.

10...Qc7 11.Nb3 Nd4

Better is 11...b6 12.Bf4 Qb7 13.Ne5

Bb7 14.Nc4. If 13.Ne5, then 13...Bd7. Or if 13.d4, then either 13...c4 or 13...Rd8. Now Black is in a lot of trouble.

12.Bf4 Qb6

If 12...Nxf3+, then 13.Qxf3 e5 14.Be3 winning the c-pawn.

13.Ne5

Threatening 14.Nc4 Qb5 15.a4 Qb4 16.Bd2.

13...Nxb3

If 13...Nd5, then 14.Nc4 Qc6 (14...Qb5 15.a4 Qb4? 16.Bd2) 15.Nba5 Qd7 16.Bd6 Rd8 17.Bxc5 b6 18.Bxd4 Bxd4 19.Nb3 wins. Black's best chance was 13...Bxe5 14.Bxe5 f6.

14.Nc4

An important Zwischenzug.

14...Qb5

If 14...Qd8, then 15.axb3 threatening 16.Bd6.

15.axb3 a5

16.Ra5 was threatened.

16.Bd6 Bf6

If 16...Re8, then 17.Bc7 threatening both 18.Nd6 and the a-pawn.

17.Qf3 Kg7 18.Re4

The combination that White begins with his 19th move will actually also work now.

18...Rd8

18...Rg8 or 18...g5 would have held out longer.

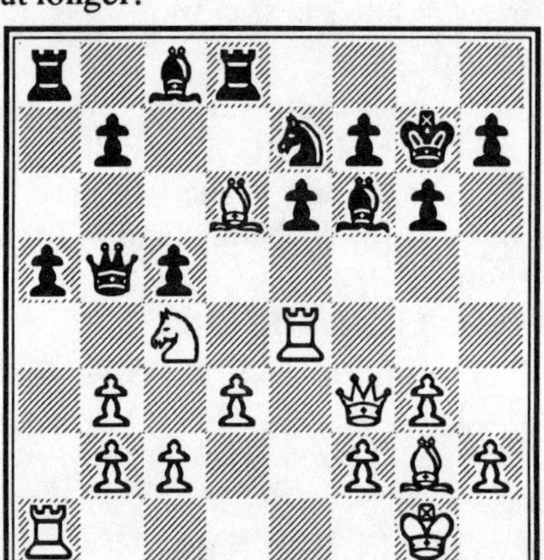

19.Qxf6+! Kxf6 20.Be5+ Kg5 21.Bg7 1-0

Black is doomed: If 21...Nf5 22.f4+ Kg4 23.Ne5+ Kh5 24.Bf3 or 21...e5 22.h4+ Kf5 (22...Kh5 23.Bf3 mate) 23.Bh3 mate.

Illustrative Game 4

GM Bobby Fischer

NM Joaquim Durao

Havana 1966

1.e4 e6 2.d3 c5 3.Nf3 Nc6 4.g3 g6 5.Bg2 Bg7 6.O-O Nge7 7.c3 O-O 8.d4 d6 9.dxc5

A strong move which makes it possible for White to advance his pawn to e5 with the usual cramping effect.

9...dxc5 10.Qe2 b6

10...e5 would prevent 11.e5, but would leave a big hole at d5.

11.e5 a5

This makes it possible to place the Bishop on the a6-f1 diagonal, but weaknesses at b5 and c4 are created of which White later takes advantage.

12.Re1 Ba6 13.Qe4 Ra7 14.Nbd2 Bd3 15.Qh4 Nd5

Exchanging Queens to avoid the coming kingside attack, but the endgame is much better for White because of Black's queenside weaknesses.

16.Qxd8 Rxd8 17.a4

It is important to fix the weaknesses before Black plays a5-a4 himself.

17...Rad7 18.Bf1

Exchanging light-squared Bishops makes it possible for White to use the holes at b5 and c4 for his own pieces.

18...Bxf1 19.Kxf1 Nde7 20.Nc4 Nc8 21.Bg5 N6e7 22.Nfd2 h6

Black probably never thought when playing this move that the h-pawn would later become a weakness that would tie him down.

23.Bxe7

The Knights are much stronger in this closed position.

23...Rxe7 24.Ra3

Fischer maneuvers his Rooks very nicely in this game to take advantage of Black's weak pawns. 25.Rb3 Rb7 26.Nxa5 is threatened.

24...Rc7 25.Rb3 Rc6 26.Ne4 Bf8 27.Ke2 Be7 28.f4 Kf8 29.g4

With Black tied down to his weak pawn at b6, White starts a second front on the kingside.

29...Ke8 30.Rf1 Rd5 31.Rf3

The other Rook pressures the weakness at h6.

31...Rd8 32.Rh3 Bf8

33.Nxa5!

After creating such a large positional advantage the inferior side can often be cracked by a tactic.

33...Rc7

Question 2: What does White do against 33...bxa5.

34.Nc4 Ra7 35.Nxb6 Nxb6 36.Rxb6 Rda8 37.Nf6+ Kd8 38.Rc6 Rc7 39.Rd3+ Kc8 40.Rxc7+ Kxc7 41.Rd7+ Kc6 42.Rxf7 1-0

Illustrative Game 5

GM Viktor Kortchnoi

GM Mikhail Botvinnik

USSR Championship, Moscow 1955

Notes in italics by Botvinnik (from *Botvinnik's Best Games, 1947-1970*: Batsford 1972).

1.Nf3 Nf6 2.g3 g6 3.Bg2 Bg7 4.O-O O-O 5.d3 c5 6.e4 Nc6 7.Nbd2 d6 8.c3

White's plan is to play d3-d4.

8...Ne8 9.Qe2 Nc7 10.Nb3 b6

Although the positioning of the Bishop at a6 looks very tempting it does not turn out too well. Probably better was 10...e5.

11.Rd1 Ba6 12.Bg5 h6 13.Be3 Kh7 14.Qc2 e5 15.d4 Qe7 16.d5

A plan worthy of approval. Black's game is cramped and in view of his Bishop at a6 and the weakness of the g-pawn he will not find it easy to get in the counter ...f5.

16...Nb8 17.a4 Nd7 18.a5

This advanced a-pawn will become a costly weakness later in the game.

18...b5 19.Nxc5

I feel Korchnoi would not have played this unless he was convinced that his opponent had overlooked the combination. The exchanges it involves are grist to Black's mill as he now frees himself from his cramped position without too much bother.

19...Nxc5 20.Bxc5 dxc5 21.d6 Qd7 22.dxc7 Qxc7 23.c4

Looks natural, but in fact White weakens his d4 square without obtaining any advantage in return. The maneuver Nd2-f1-e3 would guarantee him equality.

23...b4

Of course not 23...bxc4 because of 24.Bf1. Now it is not easy for White to realize the Knight maneuver recom-

mended previously, for example 24.Nd2 Rad8 25.Nf1 Rxd1 and White loses either his a- or his c-pawn. As Black controls c3 he only has to advance his pawn to f4 in order finally to prevent the penetration of the Knight on d5.

24.Nd2 Rad8 25.Nb3 Bf6

Necessary so as to bring his Bishop to the defense of the c-pawn. If now 26.Rd5 Rxd5 27.exd5 (27.cxd5 c4) 27...Be7 and Black will advantageously get in the advance ...f5.

26.Bf1 Bb7 27.f3 Bg5 28.Qf2 Be7 29.Be2 Kg7 30.Rxd8

White is forced to exchange both pairs of Rooks so as to simplify the position somehow and so free himself from the constant worry of defending d4.

30...Rxd8 31.Rd1 Rxd1+ 32.Bxd1 Bc8 33.Qd2 Be6 34.Be2 Bg5 35.Qd3 f5 36.Kf2 f4

Rather straightforward play. This move was better made after a preliminary ...h5 so as to render more difficult the blockade of the kingside which somewhat limits the activity of the Black Bishops.

37.g4 h5 38.h3 Be7

The blocked nature of the position reduces Black's winning chances. His hopes lie in the weakness of the White pawns on the queenside.

40.Ke1 Bh4+ 40.Kf1 Qe7

The last move before the time control. Adjournment analysis allowed me to envisage a plan of how to continue. Black's plan will be to try to infiltrate with his Queen via a4.

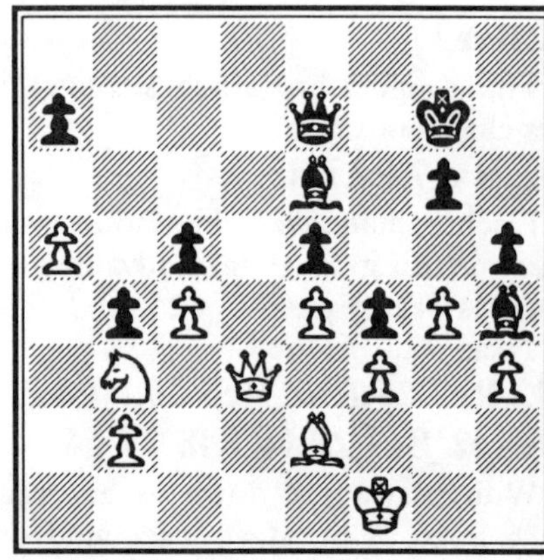

41.Qd1 Qc7 42.Qd2 Be7 43.Kg2 Qc6 44.Nc1

This move prevents 44...Qa4. Then White would play 45.Nd3 Kf6 (45...Qxa5 46.Nxe5) 46.g5+ with counterplay.

44...Qc7 45.Nb3 Bf7 46.Bf1 Kf8 47.Be2 Qc6 48.Nc1

Here too 48...Qa4 leads nowhere because of 49.Nd3. If the Black King were on c7 this maneuver would work (40...Bd6). But how can the King be transferred to the queenside? The exchange of Queens is unwise as then the ending becomes drawish. ...Bd6 is met by g5. Black has to defend his e-pawn by putting the King on f6.

48...Qc7 49.Nb3 Ke8 50.Qd1 Be6 51.Kf1 Bd8 52.Kg2 Be7 53.Kf1 Kf7 54.Kg2 Kf6 55.Qe1 Qd7 56.Qf2 Qd6

56...Qa4 is still not possible due to 57.Nxc5 Qxa5 58.Nxe6.

57.Bf1 Qc7 58.Qd2 Qc6 59.Qf2 Bf7

Now there is a real threat of 60...Qa4 61.Nxc5 Qxa5. The game would then be opened up and the Black queenside pawns supported by the Bishops would press forwards. After the following check White is no longer able to prevent the transfer of the Black King to the queenside and then ...Qa4 can no longer be prevented.

60.Qh4+ Ke6 61.Qf2 Kd6 62.Be2 Kc7 63.Bf1 Kb8 64.Qd2 Kc8 65.Qf2 Qa4

Now after 66.Qc2 Qa2 (followed by ...Be8-a4) White's pieces would occupy very passive positions. Korchnoi decides to liven up the game and to try to complicate his opponent's task.

66.Nxc5 Qxa5 67.Nd3

If 67.Nb3, then 67...Qc7 followed by ...a5 is very strong.

67...Bxc4 68.Qc2 Qc7 69.Qa4 hxg4 70.hxg4 a5 71.Qe8+ Kb7 72.Qxg6 Bd6

Not 72..a4 because of 73.Qg7 Bd6 74.Nc5+ Bxc5 75.Qxc7+ Kxc7 76.Bxc4 with an easy draw due to the opposite colored Bishops.

73.Nc5+

A tactical error as the queen ending is hopeless for White. However, it was difficult to undertake anything against the advance of the a-pawn.

73...Qxc5 74.Bxc4 Qxc4 75.Qxd6 Qe2+ 76.Kg1 Qe1+ 0-1

After the inevitable ...Qg3+ Black's material and positional advantages will be overwhelming. In this game, as in many others, I made use of the practical piece of advice which was given to me by Capablanca: "When you have the advantage and your opponent has a passive piece set-up, one should not hurry matters. With each move the likelihood of an error from the defending side increases."

Illustrative Game 6

GM Vassily Smyslov
GM Mikhail Botvinnik

USSR 1955

1.Nf3 Nf6 2.g3 g6 3.Bg2 Bg7 4.O-O O-O 5.d3 c5 6.e4 Nc6 7.Nbd2 d6 8.a4

Preventing Black from expanding on the queenside and securing the c4 square for the Knight.

8...Ne8 9.Nc4 e5 10.c3 f5 11.b4

Opening lines on the queenside.

11...cxb4

Interesting is 11...f4 threatening to expand on the kingside with ...g6-g5-g4. According to Smyslov, White should then play 12.bxc5 g5 13.h3 and if 13...h5, then 14.Nh2 threatening both 15.cxd6 and 15.Qxh5. However, 13...bxc5 is good.

12.cxb4 fxe4

The b-pawn is immune because of 12...Nxb4 13.Qb3 threatening discovered check. Good for White is 12...f4 13.b5 Nb8 14.gxf4 exf4 15.Bb2.

13.dxe4 Be6 14.Ne3 Nxb4 15.Rb1 a5

On 15...Na6, dubious is 16.Rxb7 Nc5 17.Rb4 a5. Instead Smyslov had planned 16.h4 Nc5 17.Ng5 Qe7 18.Ba3 with compensation for the pawn.

16.Ba3

When playing 11.b4 Smyslov had foreseen this position. He will win back his pawn with a slightly better position.

16...Nc7

Now Black will have trouble defending his d-pawn. According to Smyslov, correct is 16...Qe7 or 16...Rf7 with equality.

17.Bxb4 axb4 18.Rxb4 Bh6

Smyslov gives 18...Na6 19.Rxb7 Nc5 20.Rb4 Rxa4 21.Rxa4 Bb3 as better.

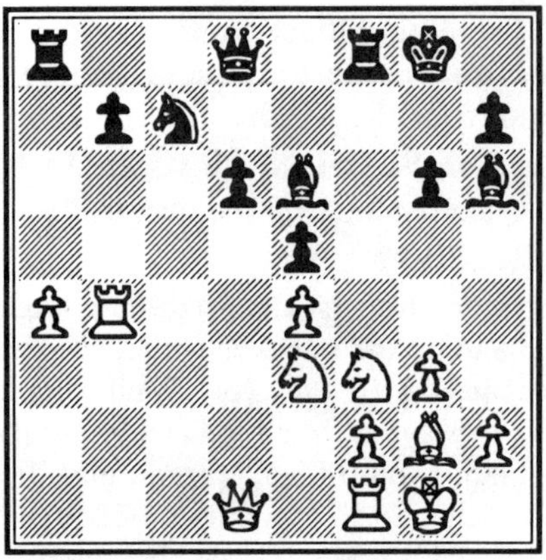

19.Rb6! Bxe3

If 19...Ra6, then 20.Rxb7 and the Knight cannot play to a6.

20.fxe3 Bc4 21.Rxd6 Qe8 22.Re1 Rf7

The a-pawn is immune: 22...Rxa4 23.Rd7 Ra1 24.Qxa1 Qxd7 25.Nxe5 Qe6 26.Rc1 b5 27.Nxc4 bxc4 28.Qd4 or 22...Qxa4 23.Qxa4 Rxa4 24.Nxe5 and White is much better in each case.

23.Ng5 Re7 24.Bf1 Bxf1

If 24...Qxa4 25.Rd8+ Re8 (25...Kg7 26.Rxa8 Qxa8 27.Bxc4+) 26.Rxa8 Rxa8 27.Bxc4+ Qxc4 28.Qd7. If 24...Ba2, then 25.Re2 is strong.

25.Rxf1

Threatening 26.Qb3+.

25...Qxa4

If 25...h6, then 26.Rff6 is strong.

26.Rd8+ Re8

If 26...Kg7, then 27.Qd6.

27.Qf3 Qc4 28.Rd7 1-0

29.Qf6 is threatened. If 28...Rf8, then 29.Nf7 threatening both 30.Qf6 and 30.Nh6+.

Illustrative Game 7

GM Tigran Petrosian
GM Gideon Stalhberg

Zurich 1953

Notes by Bronstein in italics (from *The Chess Struggle in Practice*: David McKay 1978.

The entire game is an outstanding example of Petrosian's artistry. The game's original positional design, its consistency create an integrated work of art.

It is interesting that annotators of this game, Stahlberg among them, found no noticable mistake by Black! The nuances of modern chess are so subtle that mistakes are difficult to discern even in analysis, let alone in over-the-board play.

1.e4 c5 2.d3 Nc6 3.Nf3 g6 4.g3 Bg7 5.Bg2 d6 6.O-O Nf6 7.Nbd2 O-O 8.a4 Bd7 9.Nc4 Qc8

Better is 9...Qc7. See the note to Black's 13th move.

10.Re1 Ng4 11.c3 h6 12.Qe2 Kh7 13.Nfd2 f5?

Black, fooled by his opponent's outwardly quiet development, starts a skirmish and commits a serious inaccuracy, weakening not only his kingside but also his central squares. Most approprite for him is to put his Queen on c7 instead of c8, his Rooks on e8 and d8, and gradually to prepare ...d5.

14.f4 fxe4 15.dxe4 Nf6 16.Nf3 Bg4 17.Ne3 Bh3 18.Nh4

White targets the weakness at g6.

18...Bxg2 19.Qxg2 e6 20.Qc2

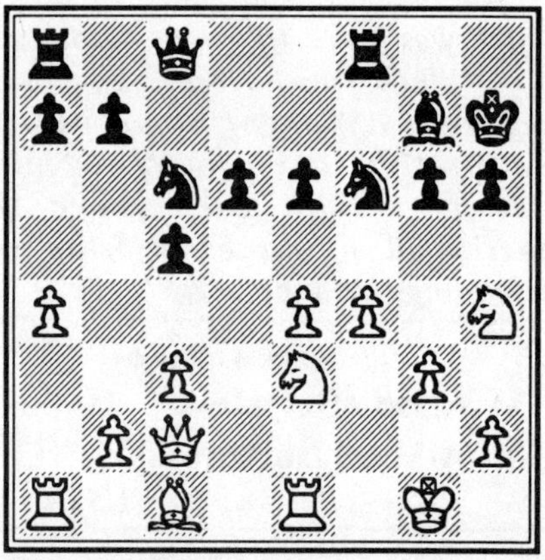

White's position uncoils like a spring. His pieces and pawns turn out to be harmoniously posted for operations in the

center and on the right. Black has weak pawns on d6 and e6. There is danger of a whirlwind's suddenly sweeping all obstacles from White's b1-h7 diagonal.

20...Ne7

Defending g6. White threatened 21.e5.

21.Nc4

Pressuring Black's other weaknesses.

21...Ne8 22.Bd2 Qc6 23.Re2 Rd8 24.Rae1 b5

Aware of White's superiority on the Kingside and in the center, Stahlberg takes his chances on the other wing, but White's position is solid enough there too.

25.axb5 Qxb5 26.Ne3 Rb8 27.Bc1 Bf6 28.Nf3 c4 29.Kg2

He is in no hurry, sure of his power.

29...Bg7 30.h4 Kg8

Removing the King from the dangerous b1-h7 diagonal.

31.Rd1 Rc8

In order to meet 32.Nd4 with 32...Qd7. If 31...Qc6, then 32.Nd4 Qc8 (or 32...Bxd4 33.Rxd4 d5 34.Ng4) 33.Qa4 is good for White.

32.e5!

Opening up the position, which White has been preparing for a long time.

32...dxe5

If 32...d5, then 33.h5 opens up the kingside.

33.Qe4!

The key move. Black is fine after 33.Nxe5 Bxe5 34.fxe5 Qc6+.

33...Rc5

If 33...exf4, then 34.Qxe6+ Kh7 (34...Rf7 35.Nd5) 35.Nd5 Nc7 36.Nxc7 Rxc7 37.Qd6 Qb7 38.Bxf4 is winning for White.

34.fxe5 Qc6

If 34...Bxe5, then 35.Ng4. In the endgame Black will not be able to defend his weak c-pawn.

35.Nc2 Qxe4 36.Rxe4 Nc6 37.Ne3 Na5

If 37...Nxe5, then 38.Nxe5 Rxe5 39.Rxe5 Bxe5 40.Nxc4 Bg7 41.Be3 a6 42.Ra1 Nc7 43.Bb6 and White wins the a-pawn and the game.

38.Nd2 Nc7 39.Nexc4 Rd8 40.Rde1 Nxc4 41.Nxc4 Nd5 42.Nd2 Rb8 43.Ra4 Rc7 44.Nf3 Nb6 45.Rg4 Kh7 46.Nd4 Re8

Black has lost a pawn and his weaknesses remain, so a victory for White is quite natural. A certain accuracy is required, however: the Queenside pawns must by reinforced, and, if absolutely necessary, the e-pawn can be given up in exchange for the a-pawn in order to form two connected passed pawns more quickly. The following moves are directed towards this end.

47.Rge4 a6 48.R1e2 Nd7 49.Nf3 Rb8 50.Be3 Bf8 51.Ra4 Rc6 52.Bd4 Rb5 53.b4 Bg7 54.Rea2

Because of tactics, White realizes his goal of exchanging his e-pawn for Black's a-pawn.

54...Nxe5 55.Nxe5 Bxe5 56.Bxe5 Rxe5 57.Rxa6 Rxa6

Not 57...Rxc3 58.Ra7+ Kg8 59.Ra8+ Kf7 60.R2a7+ Kf6 61.Rf8#. Now White wins easily with his two connected passed pawns.

58.Rxa6 Kg7 59.c4 Kf6 60.b5 Re2+ 61.Kf3 Rc2 62.Rc6 Rc3+ 63.Kf4 Rc1 64.b6 Rb1 65.g4 Ke7 66.Ke5 Re1+ 67.Kd4 1-0

Illustrative Game 8

GM Vladimir Kramnik

GM Visvanathan Anand

Moscow Quickplay 1994

1.Nf3 c5 2.g3 g6 3.Bg2 Bg7 4.O-O Nc6 5.d3 Nf6 6.e4 O-O 7.Re1 d6 8.Nc3 Bg4

A common maneuver in this type of position. Black exchanges his Bishop for the Knight to strengthen his control of the d4-square.

9.h3 Bxf3 10.Bxf3 Rb8

Another common maneuver. Black prepares to gain space on the queen-side.

11.Bg2 b5 12.a3 Nd7 13.e5

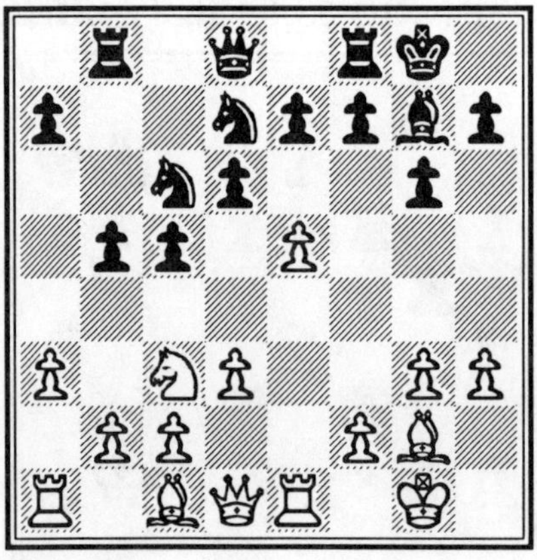

13...Nd4

Question 3: Why can't Black play 13...Ncxe5?

14.exd6 exd6 15.Nd5 Nb6

White's strong Knight needs to be removed.

16.Ne7+

Safer is 16.c3. This was the final game of a big money knockout tournament. The winner receiving $30,000, the loser $20,000.

16...Kh8 17.Bg5?

Again its safer to play 17.c3 Re8 (not 17...Ne6? 18.Nc6) 18.Bg5 f6 19.cxd4 Rxe7 20.Be3.

17...Qd7

Now the advanced Knight has no way of escaping.

18.Be3

Not 18.Nd5? Nxd5 19.Bxd5 Qf5 forking the two Bishops, nor 18.c3 Ne6 19.Bc6 Qc7 20.Qd2 Nc8! 21.Nxc8 Qxc6 22.Ne7 Qb7 23.c4 bxc4 24.dxc4 Nd4 with a winning advantage.

18...Ne6 19.Nc6 Rbc8 20.d4

White sacrifices a pawn to avoid giving up two pieces for a Rook. Also bad is 20.Na5 Bxb2.

20...Rxc6 21.d5 Rcc8 22.dxe6 fxe6 23.Bf4 e5 24.Be3 d5

Black's powerful pawn center is unstoppable.

25.b4 d4 26.Bg5 c4 27.Qd2 Qf5 28.h4 Na4 29.Be4 Qf7 30.h5 gxh5 31.Bg2 Nc3 32.Rf1 e4 33.Rae1 Qg6

Threatening 34...e3 winning a piece.

34.Be7 Rf7 35.Bc5 d3 36.cxd3 cxd3 37.Kh2 h4 38.Qe3 Re8 39.Bd4 Bxd4 40.Qxd4+ Qg7 41.Qe3 Nd5 42.Qc5 Nf6 43.Bh3

If 43.Qxb5, then 43...hxg3+ 44.fxg3 Rg8 wins.

43...Rg8 44.Qd6 Rc7

Threatening 45...Rc2.

45.Rc1 Rxc1 46.Rxc1 hxg3+ 47.fxg3 e3 48.Be6 d2 49.Rg1 Ne4 50.Qf4 e2 51.Bxg8 e1=Q 52.Bd5 Qf2 53.Qxf2 Nxf2 0-1

Illustrative Game 9

IM Octav Troianescu

GM Tigran Petrosian

Bucharest 1953

1.e4 c5 2.Nf3 d6 3.d3 Nc6 4.Nbd2 g6 5.g3 Bg7 6.Bg2 e6 7.O-O Nge7 8.Re1 O-O 9.c3 b6 10.Nf1 Ba6 11.d4 cxd4 12.Nxd4?!

Much better is 12.cxd4, keeping his pawn center.

12...Ne5 13.Bg5 h6 14.Qa4 Bb7 15.Bxe7 Qxe7 16.Rad1 Rfc8 17.Ne3 Rc5 18.f4 Nc6?

Petrosian blunders, cutting off the retreat of his Rook. Better is 18...Nd7.

19.Nxc6?

But White does not jump at the opportunity. Better is 19.Nb3.

19...Bxc6 20.Qc2 Rd8 21.Qe2 Qb7 22.Nc2 b5 23.Rd2 Rc4 24.a3 a5 25.Ne3 Rxe4

Petrosian is well-known for his positional Exchange sacrifices.

26.Bxe4 Bxe4 27.Nc2 d5 28.Nd4 b4 29.cxb4 axb4 30.a4

Better is 30.axb4.

30...Qa7 31.Qf2

31...Rc8

Question 4: Why not 31...Qxa4.

32.b3 Bf8 33.Nb5 Qa6 34.Qe2 Qb6+ 35.Kf1 Rc3 36.Nxc3

If 36.Nd4, then 36...Bc5 37.Red1 Bxd4 38.Rxd4 Bf3 wins.

36...bxc3 37.Rc2 Qxb3 38.Rec1 Bb4 39.g4 Bxc2 40.Rxc2

If 40.Qxc2, then 40...Qc4+ and 41...Qxf4.

40...Qxa4 41.f5 exf5 42.gxf5 g5 43.h4 Bc5 44.hxg5

Not 44.Rxc3 Qa1+ 45.Qe1 Qxe1+ 46.Kxe1 Bb4.

44...Qf4+ 45.Ke1 Qg3+ 46.Kd1 Qg1+ 47.Qe1 Qxe1+ 48.Kxe1 hxg5 49.Ke2 Bd4 50.Ra2 Kg7 51.Kd3 Be5 52.Ra5 Kf6 53.Rxd5 Kxf5 54.Ke3 f6 55.Rc5 Kg4 56.Rc4+ Kg3 57.Ke4 g4 0-1

After 58.Kf5 Kf3 59.Rxg4 Ke3 White will have to give up his Rook to stop the c-pawn.

Part 2

1.Nf3 Nf6 2.g3

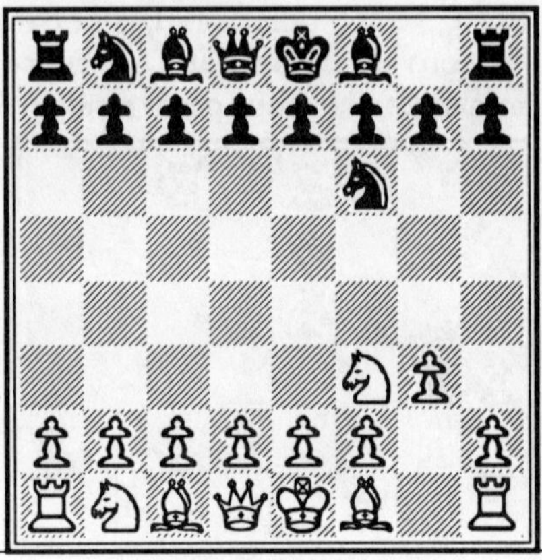

Illustrative Game 10

GM Tigran Petrosian
IM Mikhail Yudovich

Moscow 1953

1.Nf3 Nf6 2.g3 g6 3.Bg2 Bg7 4.O-O O-O 5.d3 d6 6.e4 e5 7.Nbd2 Nc6 8.Nc4 Be6

Not a good square for the Bishop.

9.Ng5 h6

Otherwise White plays 10.f4.

10.Nxe6 fxe6

The weakness at e6 is now easily defended, but Black will have to worry about it for the rest of the game.

11.c3 Kh7 12.Ne3 Qe7 13.f4 Nd8 14.a4 c6 15.fxe5 dxe5

Now Black has two weak pawns to worry about. White will slowly gain space and improve the position of his pieces before directing his attention to the weaknesses.

16.b4 Nf7 17.Qe2 Rad8 18.Nc4 Qd7 19.Rf3 Ne8 20.Qf2 b6 21.a5 b5

This avoids the opening of the a-file, but a fresh weakness at c5 is created.

22.Nd2

The Knight heads to b3 where it threatens to occupy a powerful outpost at c5.

22...Ned6 23.Qe2 Ng5 24.Re3 h5 25.h4 Ngf7

Black, on the other hand, is not able to effectively coordinate his pieces. This is due to his poor pawn structure.

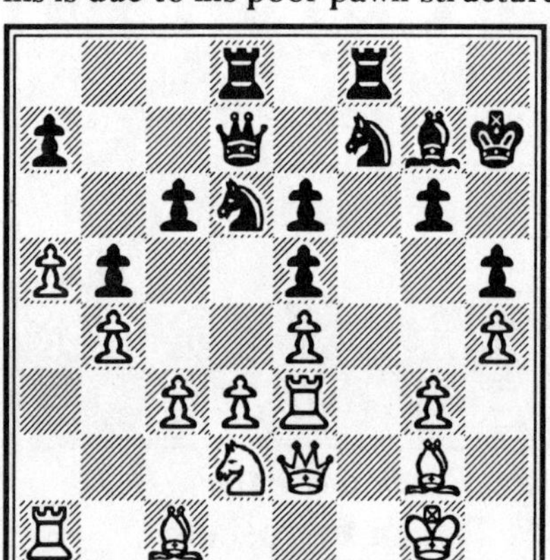

26.Nb3 Qe7 27.Rf3 Nh6 28.Bg5 Bf6 29.Rxf6 Rxf6 30.Bh3 Ne8 31.Nc5 Ng7 32.Qe3 Nf7 33.Bxf6 Qxf6 34.Rf1

Now that White has gained control of the f-file, he will be able to infiltrate and Black will not be able to defend his weaknesses.

34...Qe7 35.Qf2 Nh6 36.Qf6 Qxf6 37.Rxf6 Rd6 38.Rf8 1-0

Illustrative Game 11

GM Miroslav Filip

GM Tigran Petrosian

Amsterdam 1956

1.Nf3 Nf6 2.g3 d6 3.Bg2 e5 4.d3 g6 5.O-O Bg7 6.e4 O-O 7.Nbd2 Nbd7 8.a4 a5 9.Nc4 Nc5 10.Be3

This threatens 11.Ncxe5, but otherwise the Bishop is not well placed here. Perhaps better is 10.b3, with the idea of choosing the same plan that Black did in this game.

10...Ne6 11.h3 b6 12.Qd2 Ba6 13.b3 Nh5 14.c3

Better is 14.Ng5. Black will now soon play the strong move ...f5.

14...Qe7

Not 14...f5 15.exf5 gxf5 16.Ng5.

15.b4 f5! 16.exf5

16...f4 was threatened.

16...gxf5 17.Ng5 f4 18.Nxe6 Qxe6

Not 18...fxe3? 19.Nxe3 Qxe6 20.Bd5.

19.b5

If 19.Bxa8, then 19...Rxa8 (not 19...fxe3 20.Qe2) 20.gxf4 exf4 21.Bxf4 Rf8 22.Bh2 Qg6+ 23.Bg3 Rf3. 19.Qe2 offered the best chances. Petrosian then intended 19...Bxc4 20.Bxa8 (20.dxc4 e4 21.Qxh5 fxe3) 20...Rxa8 21.Qxh5 (21.bxa6 Qg6 22.Bd2 fxg3 23.f3 exd3) 21...Bxd3 22.Rfd1 Bc2 23.Rdc1 Bg6 24.Qf3 e4 25.Qxf4 axb4 with advantage to Black.

19...f3

The key move of the combination. Not 19...fxe3 20.Nxe3 and Black will either lose his Queen Bishop or Queen Rook.

20.bxa6 fxg2 21.Kxg2 d5

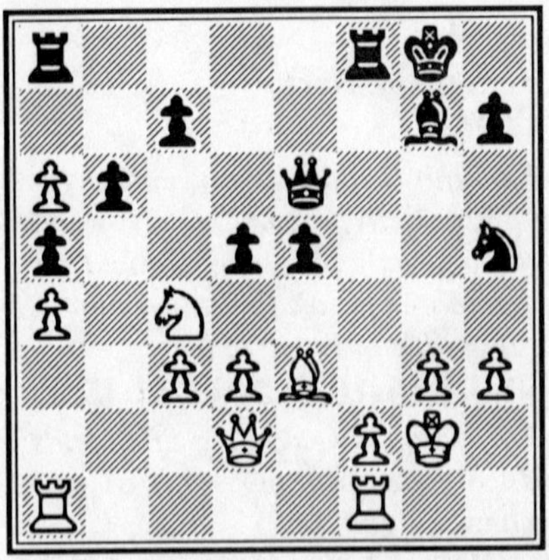

This is the position that Petrosian envisioned before playing his 15th move. Black has a great advantage due to his strong center and White's passive pieces and weakened pawn structure.

22.Na3 Rxa6 23.Qe2 Qg6 24.Kh2

Better was 24.Qg4. Now Black brings his last piece into play and prepares a breakthrough in the center.

24...Raa8 25.Nc2

Better would have been 25.Rae1 followed by 26.Nb1 and Nd2.

25...Rae8 26.Rae1 c5 27.Rg1 Nf6

Question 5: Black had a faster way to end the game here. Can you find it?

28.Qd2 d4 29.cxd4 cxd4 30.Bg5 Nd5 31.Rg2

31.Re4 would have held out longer.

31...Rf3 32.Re4 Nc3 33.Rg4 h5 34.Rh4 Rxd3 35.Qc1 Rd1 36.Qb2 Rb1 0-1

Illustrative Game 12

GM Tigran Petrosian

NM Alexey Sokolsky

Kiev 1954

1.Nf3 Nf6 2.g3 b6 3.d3 d5 4.Bg2 Bb7 5.O-O e6 6.Nbd2 Be7

Better is 6...Nbd7.

7.e4 dxe4

If 7...O-O, then 8.e5 Nfd7 9.Re1 followed by the normal maneuvers: Nf1, Bf4 etc.

8.dxe4 O-O

Not 8...Nxe4? 9.Ne5 Nc5 10.Bxb7 Nxb7 11.Qf3.

9.e5 Nfd7 10.Qe2 Nc6 11.Rd1 Qc8 12.a3

To deny the Black pieces access to the b4 square. White's strategy includes restricting his opponent by controlling key squares. While in this position White can make progress only very slowly, Black can make no progress at all. This is the essense of Petrosian's style.

12...a5 13.Re1 Rd8 14.Qc4

White maneuvers his pieces into better positions. The Queen is en route to the kingside.

14...Nc5 15.b3 Bf8 16.Qf4 Rd7 17.Nf1 Qd8 18.Be3 Ne7 19.Qg4 Nf5 20.Bf4 Nd4 21.Nxd4 Rxd4 22.Bxb7 Nxb7 23.h4 Nc5 24.Nh2 Qd7?

Better is 24...Kh8 in order to meet h5 with ...h6.

25.Nf3 Rd5 26.h5 Kh8 27.h6

Creating holes in Black's kingside.

27...gxh6 28.Kg2

Preparing to transfer the Rook to the h-file.

28...Bg7 29.b4 Nb7 30.Qh4 Rg8 31.Bxh6 Bxh6 32.Qxh6 Rg6 33.Qh4 Kg7 34.Re4 Qd8 35.c4 Rd3

Not 35...Qxh4 36.Nxh4 and both Rooks are en prise.

36.Qxd8 Nxd8

Black has been able to defend his kingside, but White is winning in the endgame as the Rook at g6 is completely out of play and Black will not be able to defend his queenside weaknesses. Slighly better was 36...Rxd8, although White is better after 37.Rd4 Rc8

(37...Rxd4 38.Nxd4 Kf8 39.Nc6) 38.Nh4.

37.bxa5 bxa5 38.Rd4

Exchanging Black's only active piece.

38...Rxd4 39.Nxd4 Nb7

Better is 39...f6, reviving the Rook. Now Black loses his queenside pawns and White's passed pawns are unstoppable.

40.Rb1 Nc5 41.Rb5 Nd3 42.Rxa5 Rg5 43.Ra7 Rxe5 44.Rxc7 h5 45.Rd7 Nc5 46.Ra7 Nd3 47.a4 Re4 48.Nb5 Re2 49.Kf3 Rc2 50.Rc7 Ne5+ 51.Ke4 Re2+ 52.Kd4 Nf3+ 53.Kd3 Rxf2 54.Ke3 Rf1 55.Ke2 Nh2 56.c5 Kg6 57.c6 Rc1 58.Rc8 Kf5 59.c7 Ke4 60.Rd8 1-0

Part 3

1.Nf3 d5 2.g3

Illustrative Game 13

GM Mikhail Botvinnik

GM Ludek Pachman

Leipzig 1960

Notes in italics by Botvinnik (from *Botvinnik's Best Games, 1947-1970*).

1.g3 d5 2.Nf3 g6 3.Bg2 Bg7 4.O-O e5 5.d3 Ne7 6.Nbd2 O-O 7.e4 d4

Better is 7...Nbc6.

8.a4 f6

This move too was not called for by the present circumstances. Now White advantageously places his Knight on h4 and prepares f4, all the more since ...g5 is impossible because of Nf5.

9.Nh4 Be6 10.f4 Nd7 11.f5

Provoking a weakening of Black's g6 and so guaranteeing control of the diagonal h3-c8.

11...Bf7 12.fxg6 hxg6 13.Bh3 Nc5 14.b4 Ne6 15.Nc4 Ng5 16.Bxg5

At first sight it might seem that this eases Black's defense. In actual fact the position which soon arises with opposite-colored Bishops is favorable to White as Black's Bishop is limited in scope and his pawns weak.

16...fxg5 17.Nf3 Bxc4

The only way to defend the e-pawn, but now Black is weak on the light squares and White's Bishop is very strong.

18.dxc4 Bf6 19.Qd2 Kg7

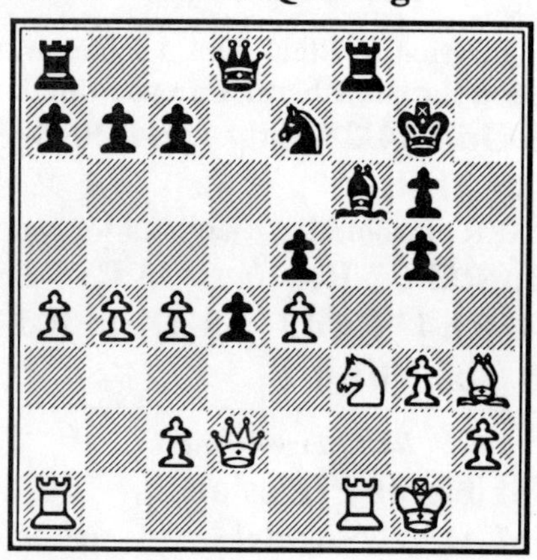

20.Ne1

Not 20.Nxg5 because after 20...Bxg5 21.Qxg5 Nc6 22.Qxd8 Raxd8 23.Rab1 Rxf1+ 24.Kxf1 a5 Black has good drawing chances in the endgame despite being a pawn down. The Knight heads to d3 where it will support the advance of the queenside pawns.

20...a5 21.Nd3

Threatening 22.Nc5 followed by Ne6+.

21...b6 22.c5

Exchanging off his doubled pawns.

22...Nc6 23.b5 Nb4

Sacrificing a pawn to exchange Knights and reduce his opponent's initiative.

24.Nxb4 axb4 25.cxb6

Question 6: Why doesn't White play 25.Qxb4?

25...cxb6 26.Qxb4 Be7 27.Qc4

Threatening 28.Rxf8 and 29.Rf1.

27...Bc5 28.Kg2 Qd6 29.Be6 Rxf1 30.Rxf1 Rf8 31.Rxf8 Qxf8 32.Qd5 Kh6

Protecting the King from checks and setting a thinly veiled trap.

33.Bg4

Not 33.Qxe5 because of 33...d3 34.cxd3 Qf2+ 35.Kh3 Qf1+ 36.Kg4 Qe2+ =.

33...Qd6

Not 33...d3 34.Qxd3 Qf2+ 35.Kh3 and Black has no more checks. Also bad is 33...Qf6 34.a5, so Black decides to exchange Queens.

34.Kf3 Kg7

Worth considering is 34...Qxd5 35.exd5 Kg7. Then White would not be able to penetrate via d5 as he does in the actual game.

35.Qxd6 Bxd6 36.Ke2 Bb4 37.Kd3 Kf6 38.Kc4 Be1 39.Kd5 Bb4

Black commits an inaccuracy allowing White's Bishop to penetrate to e8 without any difficulty. He should play 39...Bc3 so as to answer 40.Bd7 with 40...Ke7. Even so, after 41.Kc6 White is winning.

40.Bd7 Be1

If 40...Ke7, then 41.Kc6 (threatening 42.Kxb6) 41...Ba5 42.Kc7 Kf8 43.Kd8 followed by 44.Be8.

41.Be8 Bc3 42.Kc6 1-0

Black resigns in view of the following possible variation: 42...Ba5 43.Kc7 Kg7 (43...g4 44.Bd7 Kg5 45.Be6 Kh5 46.Bc4 Kg5 47.Be2 Kh5 48.h3) 44.Kd6 Kf6 45.Bxg6! This is where the weakness of the g-pawn shows itself. 45...Kxg6 46.Kxe5 Bc3 47.Ke6 g4 48.e5 Bb4 49.Kd7 Kf7 50.e6+ Kf8 51.a5.

Illustrative Game 14

GM Tigran Petrosian
GM Jan Donner

Santa Monica 1966

1.Nf3 d5 2.g3 g6 3.Bg2 Bg7 4.O-O e5 5.d3 Ne7 6.Nbd2 O-O 7.e4 c5 8.exd5 Nxd5 9.Nb3

Forcing Black to defend his c-pawn by placing his Knight on an awkward square.

9...Nd7 10.Re1 Rb8

Donner gives 10...Ne7 as better on this move or the next.

11.Nfd2 Nc7

If White now plays routinely with 12.Nc4 or 12.a4, Black solves his problems with 12...b6. White's next move prevents this.

12.Na5 Ne6 13.Nac4 Qc7

If 13...b6, then 14.Nd6 Ba6 15.a4 Qc7 (or 15...Qe7) 16.Nb5.

14.Ne4 Nb6

If 14...b6, then 15.Ned6 Ba6 16.a4 followed by 17.Nb5 with play on the queenside. Petrosian gives 14...b5 as best for Black. After 15.Ncd6 Ba6 16.a4 b4 (not 16...f5 17.axb5 fxe4 18.Rxa6) and White has the edge because of his control of the c4 square.

15.Nc3 Bd7 16.a4

After Black's next four moves he will have a very poor position. Donner gives 16...Rfd8 as best.

16...Bc6 17.Nb5 Bxb5 18.axb5

Nxc4 19.dxc4 b6

Better would have been 19...Qb6. White now has a very dominating position because of his control of the h1-a8 diagonal and the backward a-pawn which White will pressure with his major pieces.

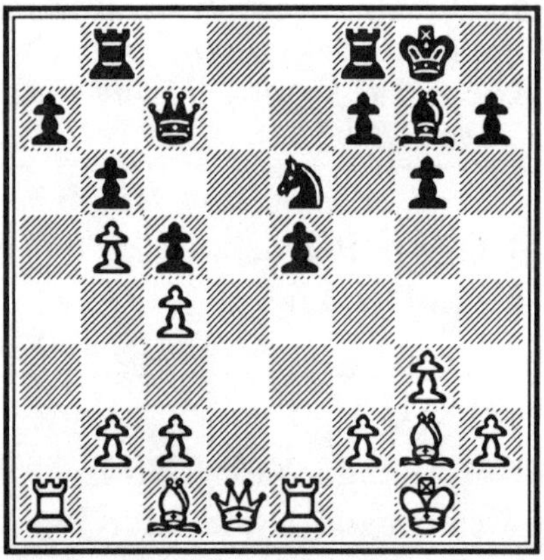

20.c3 Rfe8 21.Ra6 Re7 22.Qa4 Rc8

Black intends to defend his a-pawn by retreating his Queen to b8. However White's next move poses Black a problem that is unsolvable.

23.Bd5

If 23...Nf8 (or 23...Nd8), then 24.Bg5 followed by Ra1. Hence Black must either allow his e-pawns to be doubled or lose his a-pawn.

23...Qb8 24.Bxe6 fxe6

Black would have had better chances by giving up his weak a-pawn with 24...Rxe6.

25.Qd1

White switches his attack to the other side of the board. He intends to advance his h-pawn to give Black yet another pawn weakness.

25...Rd8 26.Qg4 Ree8 27.h4 Rd7 28.h5 gxh5 29.Qxh5 Rf8 30.Qg4 Rf6

30...Rf5 followed by ...h5 offers Black better chances according to Petrosian. White now slowly improves the position of his pieces until one of the weaknesses falls. He would like to exchange Bishops as then the pawn on e5 would be indefensible.

31.Be3 Rg6 32.Qe4 Bf8 33.Raa1 Bd6 34.Red1 Rgg7 35.Rd2 Bf8 36.Rxd7 Rxd7 37.Qg4+ Kf7 38.Qh3 Kf6

Black must bring his King into the open to defend his weaknesses.

39.Rf1

Simpler would have been 39.Qh5 followed by 40.Bg5+ and 41.Bh6+.

39...Qe8 40.Qh4+ Kg7 41.Bh6+ Kg8 42.Bxf8 Kxf8

Or 42...Qxf8 43.Qg4+ Kf7 44.Qh5+ Kf6 45.Re1. The pawn on e5 falls and Black will still have weaknesses at e6 and h7 as well as an open King.

43.Re1 Qf7 44.Rxe5 Qg6 45.Kg2 Qf7 46.Re4 Ke8 47.Rf4 Qe7 48.Qh5+ Kd8 49.Qe5 Kc8 50.Qe4 Kb8 51.Rh4 Qf7 52.Rf4 Qe7 53.Qf3 Qd6 54.Rf8+ Rd8 55.Rf6 1-0

If 55...Rd7, then 56.Qe4 Re7 57.Rf8+ Kc7 58.Qa8.

Part 4

1.Nf3 d5 2.g3 Nf6 3.Bg2 Bf5 4.O-O e6 5.d3

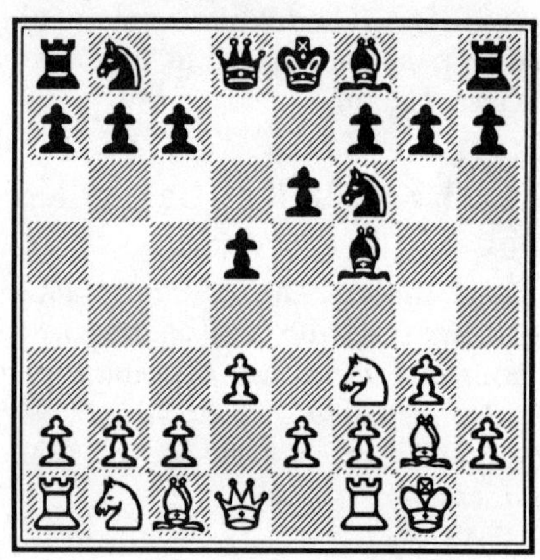

Illustrative Game 15

GM Vassily Smyslov

GM Max Euwe

Zurich 1953

Notes in italics by David Bronstein (from *The Chess Struggle in Practice*: Batsford 1980).

1.Nf3 Nf6 2.g3 d5 3.Bg2 Bf5 4.O-O Nbd7 5.d3 c6 6.Nbd2 h6

Having reinforced the d-pawn by 5...c6, more appropriate is to occupy the center with the e-pawn by 6...e5. The problem with the text move is that with his KB still blocked by his own pawns Black will not soon be able to castle short. Smyslov exploits this circumstance by 7.e4!, rather later than Morphy would have played it but with no less effect.

7.e4 dxe4 8.dxe4 Nxe4 9.Nd4 Nxd2

Can it be fear of losing the two Bishops that keeps former World Champion Euwe from playing 9...Nd6 and prompts him to develop another of his opponent's pieces? After 9...Nd6 10.Nxf5 Nxf5 11.Re1 g6 12.Ne4 or 11...e6 12.Bh3 Nd6 13.Qh5, White would still have to demonstrate the soundness of his pawn sacrifice.

10.Bxd2 Bh7 11.Bc3

An interesting idea is 11.Nxc6 bxc6 12.Bxc6 Bf5 (12...Rc8 13.Ba5) 13.Qf3 Rc8 14.Ba4.

I have no doubt that in those chess days of long ago, before the subtle methods of modern positional play had been fully worked out and when it was considered bad form to have an extra pawn or piece, White would have sacrificed his Knight on c6 without much hesitation and forced open the precarious sanctuary of the Black King.

11...Qc7

Black is not able to castle kingside: if 11...e6 12.Re1 Be7 13.Nxe6 fxe6 14.Bxg7 Rf8 15.Qh5+ with a very strong attack.

12.Qf3 e5 13.Rfe1 O-O-O 14.Nb3 f6

Euwe sets up a pawn chain on the dark squares, totally unconcerned about how to protect the light squares. Smyslov soon exploits this circumstance perfectly. 14...f5 should be played at once.

15.Ba5 Nb6

Black overestimates his position and too inflexibly refuses to make any concession. He should play 15...b6 16.Bc3 Nc5. Although White would get some chances after 17.Nxc5 Bxc5 18.a4 Bd4 19.a5, etc., the risks would be reciprocal; now there is no danger for White.

16.c4 Rd3 17.Qh5 Qe7 18.Bf1 g6 19.Qe2 Rd7 20.Qe3 Kb8 21.Rad1 Nc8

If 21...Bg8, then 22.Bxb6 axb6 23.Qxb6 followed by 24.Na5.

22.Bh3

As a consequence of 14...f6? instead of the immediate ...f5, Black's c8-h3 diagonal is very weak. He is now forced to move his pawn to f5, but this is only of partial help.

22...Rxd1 23.Rxd1 f5 24.Bb4

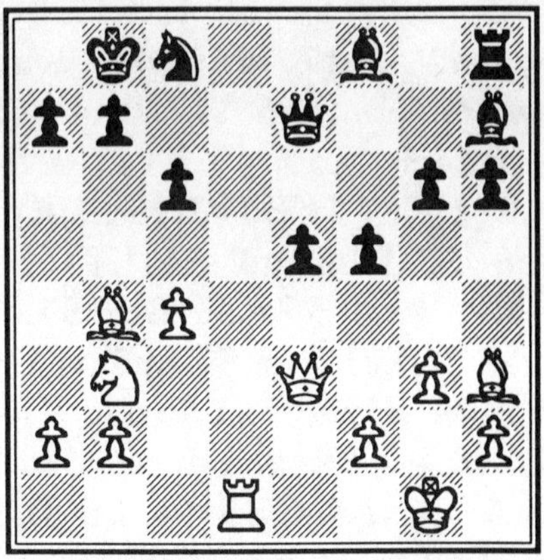

Beginning a series of combinational blows. White first exposes Black's insufficiently protected e-pawn and second his weak h-pawn: 24...Qc7 25.Bxf8 Rxf8 26.Qxh6.

24...Qf6 25.Bc3 Bg7

Yet another concession by Black. The Bishop relinquishes control of c5.

26.Nc5 Ka8

If 26...Nb6, then 27.Rd7.

27.Nxb7 Kxb7 28.Rd7+ Ka8

Not 28...Kb8 29.Rxg7 Qxg7 30.Bxe5+.

29.Qc5

The threat is 30.Bxe5 Qxe5 31.Qxc6+.

29...Nb6

Question 7: What does White do on 29...Re8

30.Rxg7 Qxg7 31.Bxe5 Qd7 32.Bxh8

An extra pawn with the two Bishops foretells the outcome of the game. The next phase is not particularly interesting; Smyslov could play more accurately in places, and, in particular, he should not allow the exchange of Queens.

32...Kb7 33.Bd4 Qe6 34.Bf1 Bg8 35.b3 f4 36.a4 fxg3 37.hxg3 Bf7 38.a5 Nc8 39.Bg2

Winning immediately is 39.a6+ Kxa6 40.Qb4 followed by 41.c5+.

39...Qd6 40.a6+ Kxa6 41.Bxc6 Qxc5 42.Bxc5 Nb6 43.Kf1 Be6 44.Ke2 Nd7 45.Bd4 Ka5 46.Bc3+ Kb6 47.Be4 g5 48.Bd4+ Ka5 49.Bxa7 Kb4 50.Bc2 Kc3 51.Bd1 Ne5 52.Ke3 Nc6 53.Bb6 g4 54.Kf4 h5 55.Be3 Na5 56.Ke5 Bc8 57.c5 Nxb3 58.Be2 Na5 59.Bb5 Nc4+ 60.Kf4 Nxe3 61.fxe3 Kb4 62.Be8 h4 63.gxh4 Kxc5 64.h5 g3 65.Kxg3 Kd5 66.h6 Bf5 67.Kf4 Bh7 68.Kg5 1-0

Illustrative Game 16

IM Bobby Fischer

IM Rudolfo Cardoso

New York 1957

1.Nf3 Nf6 2.g3 d5 3.Bg2 Bf5 4.O-O e6 5.d3 Bd6

The Bishop is misplaced here. White will later threaten e4-e5.

6.Nbd2 h6

This allows White an immediate shot. But if 6...c6, then 7.Re1 threatening 8.e4.

7.e4 Bg4

If 7...dxe4, then 8.dxe4 Nxe4 (8...Bxe4 9.Nxe4 Nxe4 10.Nd4 Nc5 11.b4 Be5 12.c3) 9.Nh4 and White is much better.

8.h3 Bxf3 9.Nxf3 Nbd7

The e-pawn is still immune because the h1-a8 diagonal will be opened.

10.Qe2 dxe4 11.dxe4 Bc5 12.e5 Nd5 13.c4 Ne7 14.Bd2 Nf5

Threatening 15...Nxg3.

15.Kh2 c6

15...a5 was better, according to Fischer.

16.b4 Be7 17.Bc3 g5

Needlessly creating more weaknesses.

18.Nd2 Qc7 19.Ne4 Rg8

Not 19...Nxe5. Then either 20.f4 or 20.Nxg5 would be decisive.

20.c5 Kf8

20...Nxe5 still loses because of 21.Nd6+. White's advantage is decisive because of the hole at d6 and Black's unsafe King position.

21.Nd6 b6 22.Nxf5 exf5 23.e6

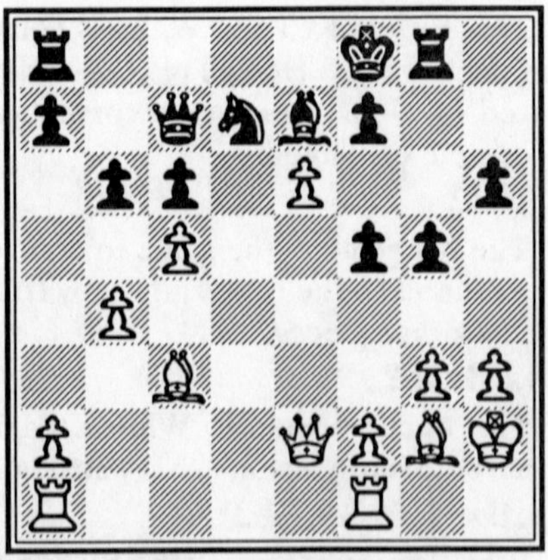

The decisive breakthrough. All of White's pieces will be attacking.

23...Bf6 24.Rad1 Ne5 25.Rfe1 Ng4+ 26.hxg4 Bxc3 27.Rd7 Qc8 28.Rxf7+ Ke8 29.Rd1 Rg7 30.Rxg7 Bxg7 31.gxf5 Kf8 32.e7+ 1-0

Illustrative Game 17

GM Tigran Petrosian
GM Max Euwe

Zurich 1953

Notes by Bronstein in italics (ibid).

1.Nf3 Nf6 2.g3 d5 3.Bg2 Bf5 4.d3 e6 5.Nbd2 h6 6.O-O Bc5

The Bishop is not well placed here, as will be seen on White's eleventh move.

7.Qe1

This move not only supports e2-e4, but also a few moves later b2-b4. Petrosian prefers 7.e4 immediately, giving the following variation: 7...dxe4 8.dxe4 Bxe4 (8...Nxe4 9.Nh4) 9.Nxe4 Nxe4 10.Qxd8+ Kxd8 11.Ne5. 8...Bh7 would be better.

7...O-O 8.e4 dxe4? 9.Nxe4 Nxe4?

Black's last moves seem rather inconsistent to me. He should have formed at least some plan by the 10th move. The first question for Black to decide is whether to keep his QB or allow it to be exchanged. If he wants to trade, he should take on e4 not with the Knight, but with the Bishop—for a long time to come he will have no convenient opportunity to trade the Bishop for more than a pawn. But if he does not want to trade, which judging by his 5th move is precisely the case, then on the last move the Bishop should have retreated to h7, maintaining the pawn tension in the center and limiting the mobility of White's d-pawn and e-pawn, and in part even his c-pawn. If now, after 9.Nxe4, Black puts his dark-square Bishop on e7, then after 10.Nh4! Black will have to give up one of his Bishops anyway, since 10...Bh7 cannot be played in view of 11.Nxf6+ and Bxb7. Bronstein's comment about creating a plan at this stage in the game is one of the most important and difficult concepts to learn for those who want to become masters. Even former World Champions are not free of fault and in this game Black gets punished for his planlessness.

10.dxe4 Bh7 11.b4 Be7 12.Bb2 Na6?

Black's carelessness has led to difficulties for him, although they are not excessive. He has to develop his Knight from b8 and find a good square for his Queen. The very best way to solve this problem is by ...c6, ...Qc7, and ...Nd7. The transfer of the Knight to c7 seems artificial, and it is hard to guess what advantage Dr. Euwe saw in it. Black was hoping to simplify the game by exchanges on the d-file.

13.a3 c6 14.Rd1 Qc8 15.c4 Nc7 16.Qc3

Now White's advantage is clear. All six Black pieces are passive, and the standard exchanges on the d-file will not ease his situation, since the absence of the hemmed-in Bishop on h7 will be felt all the more as the number of pieces is reduced. The choice of plan to realize White's advantage is a matter of taste: there are already several possibilities.

16.c5 followed by the transfer of the Knight via c4 to d6 is not bad. However, White seems to start playing hesitantly. Petrosian gives 16.c5 or 16.e5 as correct.

16...Bf6 17.Ne5 Rd8 18.Bf3

White intended 19.Bh5 but this is hardly a dangerous threat.

18...Ne8 19.Rxd8 Qxd8 20.Rd1 Qc7 21.c5 a5 22.Bg2 axb4 23.axb4 Rd8 24.Rxd8 Qxd8 25.Qc2 Nc7 26.Bf1? Nb5 27.f4

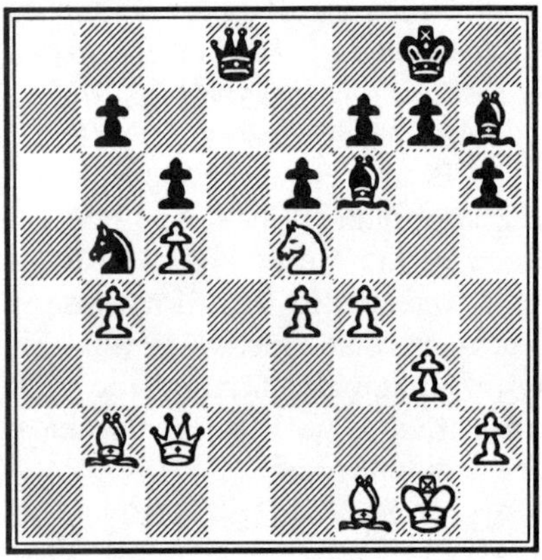

White has not maneuvered very energetically. Black has been able to improve the position of his pieces, but his basic problem remains unsolved: his Bishop on h7 is out of play. This has made White careless – he has completely stopped worrying about his e-pawn, and now Black has a chance to punish him. With 27...Qa8, threatening to burst into a2, Euwe can approximately equalize the chances. Therefore, instead of 26.Bf1 and 27.f4, extending the scope of Black's QB, the more restrained 26.f3! would have been correct. One of the techniques for freeing a hemmed-in Bishop on the kingside is ...f6 and ...e5, clearing a path for the Bishop via g8. This is what Black now intends to do. White is forced to operate actively if he wants to keep his advantage.

27...Kf8?

If 27...Nd4, then 28.Qd1 Nb5 29.Qxd8+ Bxd8 30.Bd3 Kf8 31.Kf2 f6 32.Nc4 Ke7 33.Ke3 and White is better in the endgame. He will play e4-e5 followed by Nd6. 27...Qa8 is correct, as Bronstein explained.

28.Kf2

The King enters the game to control key squares in the center, thereby freeing his other pieces.

28...Bxe5?

The decisive error. White's dark-squared Bishop becomes very strong.

29.Bxe5 f6 30.Bb2

White's plan is to play the Bishop to c4, the King to e3, and then with the advance of the g-pawn to create weaknesses at f6 and g7.

30...Ke7 31.Bc4 Bg6 32.Ke3 Bf7 33.g4 Qc7 34.e5

Incorrect is 34.g5 hxg5 35.fxg5 fxg5 36.Bxg7 Qf4+.

34...Qd8 35.exf6+

Not 35.f5 fxe5 36.fxe6 Nd4 37.Qh7 Nxe6 38.Bxe6 Qd1! threatening perpetual check beginning with 39...Qe1+.

35...gxf6 36.h4 Nc7

Worth considering is 36...Qg8.

37.Qc3 Nd5+

Black decides to sacrifice the f-pawn to achieve opposite-colored Bishops. 37...Qh8 38.Qd4 threatening 39.Qd6+ and 39.g5 is decisive. Black would also have little hope after the passive 37...Ne8.

38.Bxd5 Qxd5 39.Qxf6+ Ke8 40.Qh8+ Kd7 41.Qg7 Ke8 42.Bf6

Black's only hope is perpetual check, but White is able to prevent this. White's pawn majority on the kingside will eventually be decisive. He plans to play h5, fixing Black's h-pawn on a dark square. But not 42.h5 immediately due to 42...Qh1 and White cannot escape perpetual check. The threat is 43.Qh8+ Kd7 44.Qd8 mate.

42...Qb3+ 43.Bc3 Qd1

43...h5 would have offered more chances.

44.Qh8+ Kd7 45.Qb8 Qc1+

If 45...Qg1+, then 46.Kd2 Qf2+ 47.Kd1 Qf1+ 48.Kc2 Qe2+ 49.Bd2 Qa6, which is a position reached in the actual game.

46.Bd2 Qg1+ 47.Kd3 Qf1+ 48.Kc2 Qa6

If 48...Bg6+, then 49.f5. If 48...Qc4+, then 49.Kb2 Qd4+ 50.Bc3 Qf2+ 51.Ka3 e5 52.Qxb7+ Ke8 53.Qxc6+ Kf8 54.Qc8+ Ke7 55.Qc7+ Kf8 56.Qd8+.

49.h5 Qa2+ 50.Kd3 Qb1+ 51.Ke2 Qe4+ 52.Kf2 Qd4+ 53.Be3 Qxb4 54.Qf8 Qb2+ 55.Kg3 Qf6 56.Qd6+ Kc8 57.Bd4

Forcing the exchange of Queens, after which White wins the h-pawn.

57...Qd8 58.Qxd8+ Kxd8 59.Bg7 Kc7 60.Bxh6 b6 61.cxb6+ Kxb6 62.Kh4 1-0

Part 5

1.Nf3 d5 2.g3 c6 3.Bg2 Bg4 4.O-O

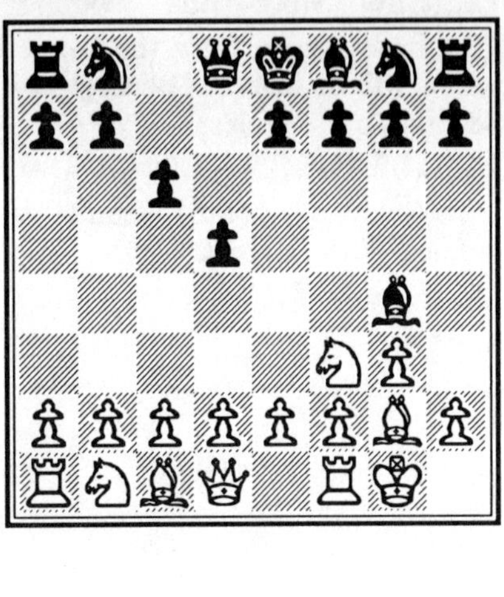

Illustrative Game 18

GM Mikhail Botvinnik
IM Gyorgy Szilagyi

Amsterdam 1966

1.g3 d5 2.Nf3 c6 3.Bg2 Bg4 4.d3 Nd7 5.h3 Bxf3

It is dubious to give up a Bishop for a Knight without compensation.

6.Bxf3 e5 7.Nd2 Ngf6 8.e4 dxe4 9.dxe4 Bc5

9...Be7 is better.

10.O-O Qe7 11.c3 O-O

Worth considering is 11...a5 to prevent White from expanding on the queenside.

12.b4 Bb6 13.a4 Rfd8

If 13...a5, then 14.bxa5 Bxa5 15.Ba3.

14.Qc2

Better is 14.Rb1.

14...Rac8

Black does not take advantage of White's lapse. Correct is 14...a5.

15.Be2

This Bishop realigns on the a2-g8 diagonal.

15...c5?

A very bad move that weakens the d5 square and further constricts Black's pieces.

16.b5 Ne8 17.Nc4 Nd6 18.Bg5!

Forcing Black to weaken the a2-g8 diagonal, because if 18...Nf6, then 19.Ne3 threatening 20.Nd5, or if 18...Qxg5, then 19.Nxd6 c4 (preventing 20.Bc4 and threatening 20...Qxg3+) 20.Kg2 Nf6 21.Rad1 Rb8 22.Nxc4.

18...f6 19.Be3 Nxc4

19...Kh8 would have offered more resistance, although Black is lost in any case.

20.Bxc4+ Kh8 21.a5 Bc7 22.Rfd1

White would like to exchange Rooks. This will make Black's defense even more difficult, as mate will later be threatened on g8.

22...Nf8 23.Qa2 Rxd1 24.Rxd1 Rd8 25.Rxd8 Bxd8 26.a6

Freeing the Queen from the defense of the a-pawn and further constricting Black's Bishop. The pawn on a7 is also very weak if White infiltrates with his Queen or in the endgame with his King.

26...b6

Just as bad is 26...bxa6 27.Qxa6 or 26...Bb6 27.Qd2 threatening 28.Qd5.

27.Kg2 Qd7 28.Qe2 Ng6

28...Ne6 would have held out longer.

29.Bb3 Ne7 30.Qc4 h6 31.Qf7

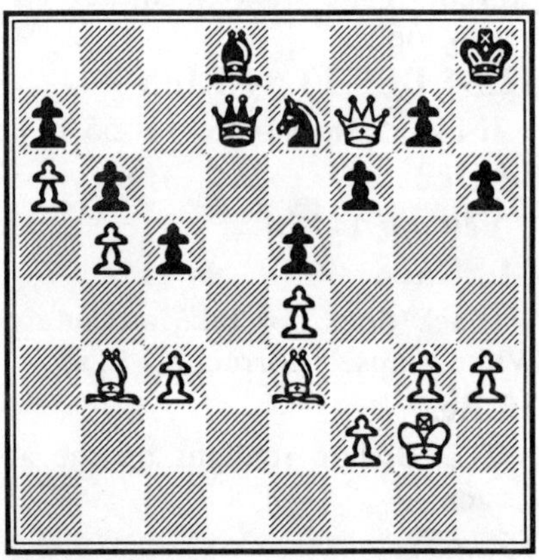

31...Kh7

Question 8: What does White do on 31...Qxb5.

32.Bc4 Qd6 33.h4 Qd1 34.Qe8

Black is helpless against 35.h5, 36.Bf7 and 37.Bg6+.

34...f5 35.exf5 Nxf5 36.Bg8+ 1-0

36...Kh8 37.Bf7+ and 38.Bg6 mate.

Part 6

1.Nf3 d5 2.g3 c5 3.Bg2

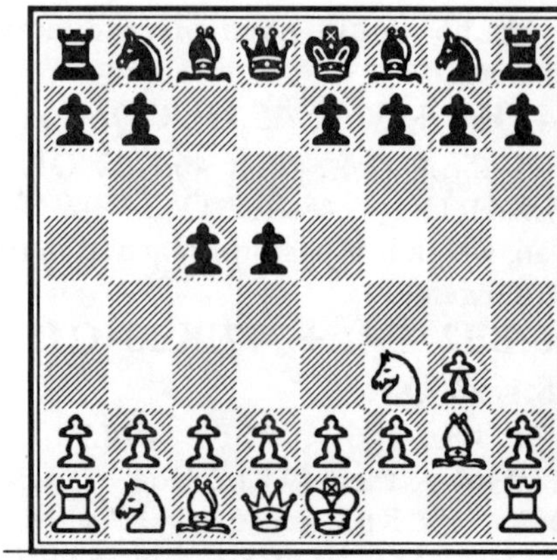

Illustrative Game 19

NM Bobby Fischer
NM Herbert Seidman

New York 1956

1.Nf3 Nf6 2.g3 c5 3.Bg2 Nc6 4.O-O e5 5.d3 d5 6.e4 Be7 7.Nbd2 O-O 8.Re1 dxe4

This pawn exchange is usually good for White because of the resulting weak d5 square. Better is 8...d4.

9.dxe4 Qc7 10.c3 b6 11.Qe2 a5

In order to play ...Ba6, but now Black has two more weaknesses at b5 and c4.

12.a4

Fixing the weakness.

12...Ba6 13.Nc4 b5

A bad move. Now the a- and c-pawns will be targets. Black's position becomes quite lifeless.

14.axb5 Bxb5 15.Bf1

In order to free the Queen from the defense of the Knight.

15...Rad8 16.Qc2

16...Ng4

Black's pieces are not engaged in coordinated, concerted action, but are merely attacking "here and there." In the middlegame, this is where most players are weak, according to Capablanca.

17.h3 Nf6 18.Nfd2

White on the other hand correctly coordinates his pieces to take advantage of Black's weaknesses on the queenside.

18...Rfe8 19.Nb3 Qc8

19...Bxc4 would only have temporarily saved a pawn. Black's position would have remained very bad.

20.Kh2 Qe6 21.Nbxa5

White has won a pawn and the outcome is not in doubt.

21...Nxa5 22.Nxa5 Bxf1 23.Rxf1 c4 24.Qe2 Rd3 25.Ra4 Red8 26.Nxc4 h6 27.Re1 Bc5 28.Kg2 g5 29.Nd2 Qd7 30.Ra5 Bb6 31.Ra6 Qb7 32.Ra1 Qd7 33.Nc4 Bxf2 34.Qxf2 Nh5 35.Nxe5 Qe6 36.Nxd3 Rxd3 37.Re3 Rd1 38.Qf3 Qb3 39.Qxh5 1-0

Part 7

1.Nf3 d5 2.g3 c5 3.Bg2 Nc6 4.O-O e6 5.d3 Bd6 6.e4 Nge7 7.Nbd2 O-O

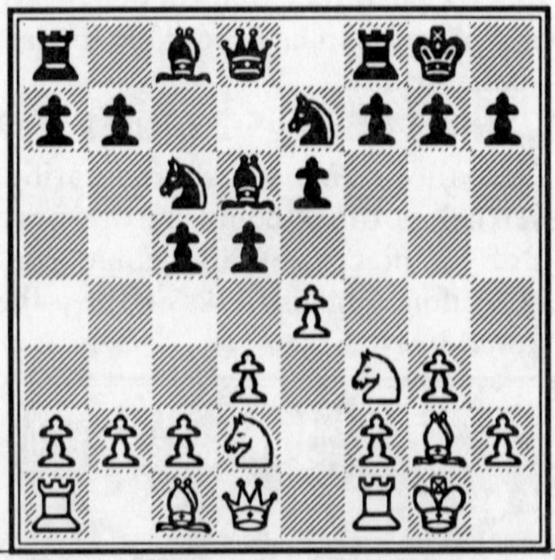

Illustrative Game 20

IM Bobby Fischer
NM Antillo Di Camillo

New Jersey 1957

1.e4 e6 2.d3 d5 3.Nd2 Bd6 4.Ngf3 c5 5.g3 Nc6 6.Bg2 Nge7 7.O-O O-O 8.Re1 Qc7 9.c3 Bd7 10.Qe2 f6

Although this move weakens the e6 square, it is necessary to prevent the e4-e5 advance. 10...Ng6 would be met with 11.h4.

11.a3

White switches his attention to expanding and opening lines on the queenside.

11...Rae8 12.b4 b6

The correct move is 12...b5. Black will now find it difficult to maneuver his pieces.

13.d4 cxd4

Opening up the position is favorable for White, but 14.e5 was threatened.

14.cxd4 dxe4 15.Nxe4 Nd5 16.Bb2 Qb8 17.Nfd2 Nd8 18.Nxd6 Qxd6 19.b5

Preparing to open the a3-f8 diagonal.

19...Bc8 20.a4 Qd7 21.Ba3 Rf7 22.Nc4 Nb7 23.Qd3

White improves the position of his pieces and creates further weaknesses in Black's position. Black's pieces are poorly placed and he is not able to start any counterplay.

23...Rd8 24.Be4 g5 25.Rac1 Ne7

This allows White a combination. Nevertheless Black could hardly move any of his pieces. White could continue by doubling his rooks on the c-file followed by Ne3.

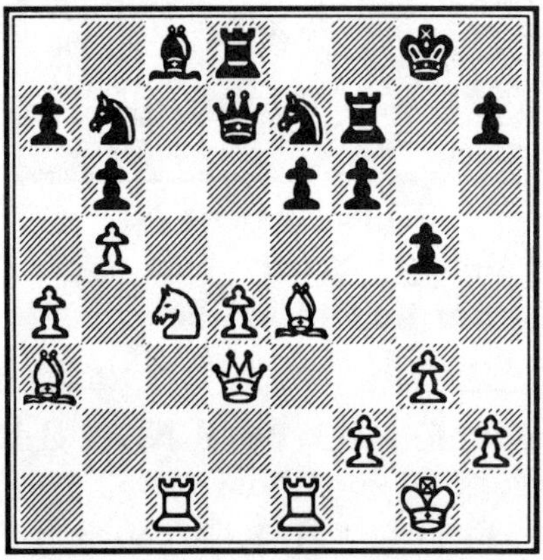

26.Bxb7 Bxb7 27.Nd6 Nf5

Black decides to sacrifice the Exchange. He has counterplay because of his control of the h1-a8 diagonal. If 27...Rg7 28.Nxb7 Qxb7 29.Rxe6 his position falls apart.

28.Nxf7 Qd5

28...Qxf7 would have offered much better chances. Black seems to have overlooked White's next move. Now White is able to force an easily winning endgame, although he must be cautious because Black could create dangerous threats against his King.

29.Qe4 Qd7 30.Qxe6 Qxe6 31.Rxe6 Kxf7 32.Ree1 Kg6 33.Rc7 Bf3 34.Bb2 h5 35.Rxa7 Rc8 36.Rc1 Re8 37.Ra6 h4 38.g4

A good move that stops Black's counterplay.

38...Bxg4 39.Rxb6 Re2 40.Bc3 h3 41.d5 Nh4 42.Rxf6+ Kh5 43.b6 Nf3+ 44.Rxf3 Bxf3 45.b7 Re8 46.Be5 Rxe5 47.b8=Q Re4 48.Qg3 Rg4 49.d6 1-0

Illustrative Game 21

GM Bobby Fischer
GM Boris Ivkov

Santa Monica 1966

1.e4 c5 2.Nf3 e6 3.d3 Nc6 4.g3 d5 5.Nbd2 Bd6 6.Bg2 Nge7 7.O-O O-O 8.Nh4 b6 9.f4 dxe4 10.dxe4 Ba6 11.Re1 c4

Better is 11...Bc7. The text move threatens to weaken White's queenside with 12...c3, but this is easily met.

12.c3 Na5 13.e5 Bc5+ 14.Kh1 Nd5

Ivkov had originally intended 14...Rc8, but was worried about 15.b4. After 15...cxb3 16.axb3, 17.b4 is threatened.

15.Ne4 Bb7 16.Qh5 Ne7

16...Qe8, threatening 17...f5, would have put up more resistance. But then 17.f5 is strong.

17.g4

Reinforcing the pawn advance f4-f5, which Black's last move prevented.

17...Bxe4

Exchanging off the powerful Knight, but a powerful Bishop takes its place. It is unlikely that Black has a defense.

18.Bxe4 g6 19.Qh6 Nd5

Black's play has been quite planless. His original intention was 19...Kh8 but he was worried about 20.Nf3, threatening 21.Ng5. Even so, this may have been his best continuation.

20.f5

Black will not be able to defend g6. Ivkov wrote that resignation would have been the best move here.

20...Re8 21.fxg6 fxg6 22.Nxg6 Qd7

If 22...hxg6 23.Qxg6+ Kf8 24.Bh6+

Ke7 25.Qg7 mate.

23.Nf4 Rad8 24.Nh5 Kh8 25.Nf6 Nxf6 26.exf6 Rg8 27.Bf4 Rxg4 28.Rad1 Rdg8

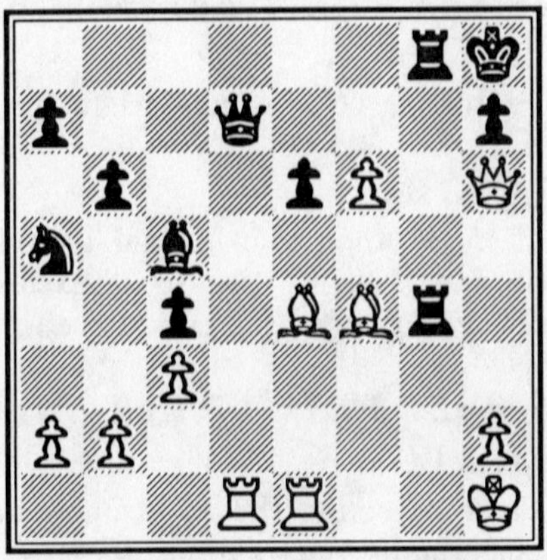

Black's last (and only) hope in this game: 29.Rxd7? **Question 9: Why didn't White play it?**

29.f7 1-0

29...Qxf7 30.Be5 + .

Part 8

1.Nf3 d5 2.g3 c5 3.Bg2 Nc6 4.O-O e6 5.d3 Nf6 6.Nbd2 Be7 7.e4

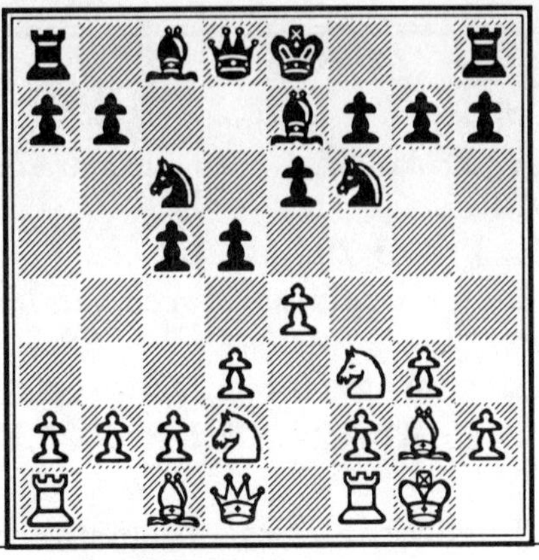

Illustrative Game 22

GM Tigran Petrosian

IM Gedeon Barcza

Stockholm 1952

1.e4 c5 2.Nf3 Nc6 3.d3 e6 4.Nbd2 d5 5.g3 Nf6 6.Bg2 Be7 7.O-O O-O 8.Re1 b6 9.e5 Ne8

Better is 9...Nd7. At e8 the Knight is passively placed and difficult to bring into play.

10.Nf1 Kh8 11.Bf4 f5

A defensive move against White's attack on the kingside.

12.h4 Nc7

Black would like to play 13...d4 followed by 14...Nd5.

13.N1d2

Now if 13...d4, then 14.Nc4 Nd5 15.Bg5 and White's Knight reaches d6. Note that if 15...b5 16.Nd6 Nxe5, then 17.Nxe5 Qxd6 18.Bxd5 followed by 19.Bxe7 wins.

13...Bb7 14.c3 b5 15.Nb3 a5 16.Bg5

Threatening 17.Nxc5.

16...Na6 17.d4 c4

If 17...cxd4, then 18.cxd4 followed by Nb3-c1-d3 where the Knight threatens to go either to c5 or f4.

18.Nc1 Nc7

Black's misplaced pieces make it difficult for him to create counterplay on the queenside.

19.Ne2

White intends to transfer his Knights to f4 and g5 where they will pressure the e6-pawn and Black's King.

19...Kg8 20.Nf4 Qe8

Better is 20...Rb8.

21.Bxe7 Qxe7 22.Ng5 g6

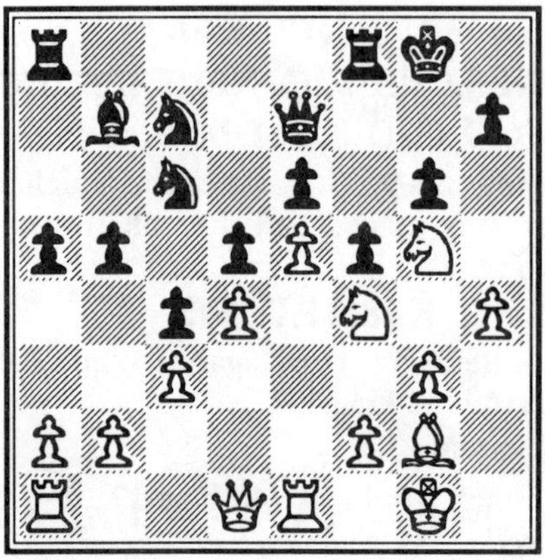

23.a4

White attacks Black's pawn structure from both sides of the board.

23...Ba6?

A blunder after which the game quickly ends. Correct is 23...b4. Petrosian intended to play 24.b3. Bad for Black would then be 24...bxc3 25.bxc4 dxc4 (or 25...Nb4 26.cxd5 Bxd5 27.Bxd5 Nbxd5 28.Ngxe6) 26.d5 c2 27.Qxc2 Nb4 28.d6 Nxc2 29.dxe7 Rfb8 30.Bxb7 Rxb7 31.Red1 Nxa1 32.Rd8+. Better is 24...cxb3 25.Qxb3 Rab8.

24.Nfxe6 Nxe6 25.Bxd5 Rad8

Or 25...Nd8 26.Bxa8.

26.Bxe6+ Kg7 27.axb5 Bxb5 28.d5 f4 29.Qg4 1-0

Illustrative Game 23

GM Tigran Petrosian
IM Gedeon Barcza

Budapest 1952

1.Nf3 Nf6 2.g3 d5 3.Bg2 c5 4.d3 Nc6 5.O-O e6 5.Nbd2 Be7 7.e4 O-O 8.Re1 b6

Better is 8...b5.

9.e5 Nd7 10.Nf1 Ba6

The Bishop is not very effective on this square. Black seems to be playing without a plan.

11.h4 Qe8

With the idea of ...Bd8-c7, putting pressure on the e5-pawn.

12.Bh3

A good move. The Bishop pressures the e6-square, preventing Black from breaking with ...f6.

12...Bd8 13.Bf4 Bc7 14.N1h2 Nd8

Protecting e6 in order to later play ...f6.

15.Qd2 d4

If 15...f6, then 16.exf6 Bxf4 17.Qxf4 Rxf6 (not 17...gxf6 due to 18.Bxe6+ Nxe6 19.Qg4+) 18.Qe3 followed by 19.Ng4.

16.Bg2 Bb7 17.Re2 Nc6 18.Rae1

Overprotecting the e5 strongpoint which cramps Black's position.

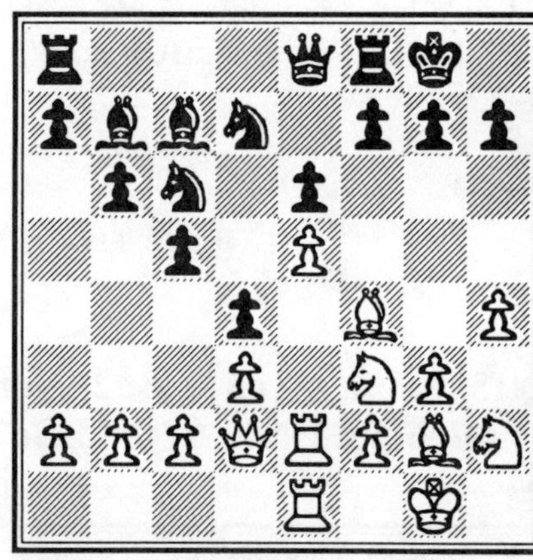

18...b5

Finally starting queenside counterplay and also threatening 19...Ba5.

19.c3 dxc3 20.bxc3 b4

Better would have been the less hasty 20...a5.

21.cxb4 Nxb4 22.Ng4 Nd5 23.Bg5 Kh8 24.Nfh2 Rb8 25.h5 f6?

The decisive error. White's pieces will now become very active. Better is 25...Bd8 26.h6 g6, although White is much better.

26.exf6 gxf6

If 26...N7xf6, then 27.h6 is strong.

27.Rxe6 Qxh5 28.Bh4

White now targets the weakness at f6.

28...Bd8 29.Rd6 N5b6 30.Bxb7 Rxb7 31.Qb2 Qf5 32.Ree6 Rb8

Black can hardly move his pieces. If 32...Kg7, then 33.a4 Rb8 34.Qd2 threatening both 35.a5 and 35.Qh6+.

33.Qe2 Bc7

This loses the f-pawn. But after Nh2-f1-e3 and Qf3 Black's position would collapse in any case.

34.Bxf6+ Nxf6 35.Rxf6 Qg5

If 35...Bxd6, then 36.Rxf5 Rxf5 37.Qe6.

36.Rxf8+ Rxf8 37.Rc6 Qg7

If 37...Bb8, then 38.Qb2+ Kg8 39.Nf6+ Kf7 40.Nxh7 or if 37...Bd8, then 38.Qe5+ Qxe5 39.Nxe5 Be7 40.Rc7.

38.Rxc5 Na4 39.Rc4 Nc3 40.Qb2 Ba5 41.Rc5 Bb6 42.Qxc3 Bxc5 43.Qxc5 Rd8 44.Ne5 Qb7 45.Nhf3 Rc8 46.Qd4 1-0

Illustrative Game 24

IM Bobby Fischer

NM Arthur Feuerstein

U.S. Championship 1957/58

Notes by Fischer in italics (from *Bobby Fischer's Games of Chess: Simon & Schuster 1959).*

1.e4 c5 2.Nf3 e6 3.g3 Nf6 4.d3 d5 5.Nbd2 Be7 6.Bg2 O-O 7.O-O Nc6 8.Re1 Qc7 9.Qe2 Rd8

Better is 9...b5.

10.e5 Ne8 11.c3

If 11.Nf1, then Fischer gives this variation: 11...Nd4 12.Qd1 (12.Nxd4 cxd4 with an open c-file) 12...Bd7 13.c3 Nxf3+ 14.Qxf3 Bc6 or ...b5 with a good game for Black.

11...b5 12.Nf1 b4 13.Bf4 Qa5

A strategic mistake. Correct is 13...bxc3 14.bxc3 Rb8. As played, Black does not obtain enough play on the queenside to counterbalance White's coming attack on the other wing.

14.c4

A double-edged move, because while designed to fix the pawn structures and reduce Black's queenside counterplay, it weakens the d4-square.

14...Nc7 15.h4

The key move to White's attack. White's plan is to (a) advance the h-pawn to h6, forcing a weakness at f6; (b) maneuver a Knight to g4; (c) trade off Black's KB. The outcome of the game depends on the execution of this plan.

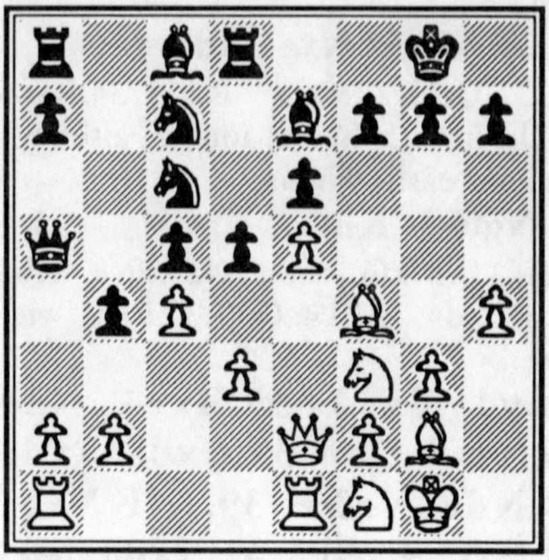

15...Qb6 16.h5 b3 17.a3 dxc4 18.dxc4 Ba6

Better is 18...Bb7 followed by 19...Nd4.

19.N1h2 Rac8 20.h6 g6 21.Bg5 Nd4 22.Qe3 Bxg5

If 22...Nc2, then 23.Qf4.

23.Qxg5 Ne8

Guarding the f6 square. If 24...Bxc4, then 25.Ng4.

24.Ng4 Nf5 25.Rac1 Qc7 26.Nd2

This Knight threatens both the b-pawn and to move to e4 aiming at the f6 square.

26...Rd4

If 26...Qb6, then 27.Ne4 is very strong.

27.Nxb3 Rxc4 28.Rcd1 Ra4

If 28...Rc2, then 29.Be4 Rxb2 30.Nf6+ or if 28...Qe7, then 29.Qxe7 Nxe7 30.Ne3 Ra4 31.Rd7 winning.

29.Re4

With the indirect plan of dislodging Black's Knight on f5.

29...Bb5 30.Rc1

In order to draw Black's Queen away from the defense of the kingside.

30...Qb6 31.Nd2

This brings White's Knight into the game with decisive effect. There is no adequate defense against 32.Rxa4 and 33.Ne4.

31...Rxe4 32.Nxe4 Bd3

32...Qd8 33.Qxd8 Rxd8 34.Rxc5 would have held out longer, although White is easily winning.

33.Ngf6+ Kh8

If 33...Nxf6, then 34.Nxf6+ Kh8 35.g4 Nd4 36.Ne4 Qd8 37.Rxc5 winning.

34.g4 Bxe4 35.Bxe4 Nd4 36.Nxe8 Qd8 37.Qxd8 Rxd8 38.Nd6 Ne2+ 39.Kf1 Nxc1 40.Nxf7+ Kg8 41.Nxd8 Nb3 42.Ke2 Nd4+ 43.Kd3 Kf8 44.Nc6 1-0

This was Fischer's first game in his first U.S. Championship, which he won at the age of 14. He played the King's Indian Attack twice in that tournament.

Illustrative Game 25

GM Bobby Fischer

NM Uzi Geller

Natanya 1968

1.e4 e6 2.d3 d5 3.Nd2 c5 4.g3 Nf6 5.Bg2 Be7 6.Ngf3 O-O 7.O-O Nc6 8.Re1 Qc7 9.e5 Nd7 10.Qe2 b5 11.h4 a5 12.Nf1 Nd4

Black opens the c-file in order to attack White's backward c-pawn. One drawback is that the pawn on d4 is permanently weak.

13.Nxd4 cxd4 14.Bf4

With this Bishop on the same diagonal as his Queen, Black must watch out for tactics beginning with Bxd5.

14...Ra6 15.Nh2

15.Bxd5 is not effective due to 15...Bb4 16.Reb1 (worse is 16.Rfc1 because of 16...exd5 17.e6 Rxe6 18.Qxe6 Qxf4 19.Qxd7 Qxc1+ winning.) 16...exd5 17.e6 Bd6 18.exd7 Bxd7 with an equal position.

15...Rc6 16.Rac1 Ba6

Necessary was 16...Qb6. Now the tactic works.

17.Bxd5 exd5

Black could offer more resistance with 17...Rc5 18.Be4 Rc8 (if 18...Nxe5, then 19.c3 threatening 20.cxd4) 19.Nf3 Rxc2 20.Rxc2 Qxc2 21.Nxd4 Qxe2 22.Nxe2 Nc5.

18.e6 Qd8

If 18...Bd6, then 19.Bxd6 Rxd6 20.exd7 Qxd7 21.Nf3 and Black cannot defend his pawn on d4.

19.exd7 Re6 20.Qg4 f5

If 20...Qxd7, then 21.Be5 wins easily. The text move weakens the e5 square which White will later use for his pieces.

21.Qh5 Qxd7 22.Nf3 g6 23.Qh6 Bf6 24.Rxe6 Qxe6 28.Be5 Bxe5 26.Re1 f4 27.Rxe5 Qd7 28.h5 fxg3 29.hxg6

29...gxf2 +

Question 10: How does White finish off the game after 29...Rxf3.

30.Kxf2 hxg6 31.Qxg6 + Kh8 32.Rh5 + 1-0

Illustrative Game 26

GM Mikhail Botvinnik

IM Wolfgang Uhlmann

Moscow 1956

Notes by Botvinnik in italics (from *Botvinnik's Best Games, 1947-1970: Batsford 1972).*

1.e4 e6 2.d3 d5 3.Nd2 Nf6 4.Ngf3 c5 5.g3 Nc6 6.Bg2 Be7 7.O-O O-O 8.Re1 Rb8

This wastes time. Better is the immediate 8...b5.

9.e5 Nd7 10.Nf1 b5 11.h4 Ba6

A loss of time. In mutual analysis after the game, Uhlmann and I established that it is correct to advance the a- and b-pawns straightaway. Subsequent tournament practice confirmed this opinion.

12.N1h2 b4 13.Bf4 Bb5 14.Bh3 c4

In principle a mistake, after which White gets a chance to solidify his strongpoint in the center, his e-pawn, whereas Black is denied all counterplay. He ought to advance his a-pawn to a3.

15.d4 Qb6 16.Be3 Rfc8 17.Ng5

Threatening 18.Nxe6.

17...Nf8 18.f4 Nd8 19.f5

Excessive haste. True, the f-file is opened but at the same time Black's pieces get a certain freedom of action. 19.g4 deserved preference.

19...exf5 20.Bxf5 Nde6

Black doesn't straightaway think of the right idea of exchanging the white-squared Bishops by means of 20...Bd7, which would reduce White's attacking chances.

21.Qf3

A controversial point. After the exchange on g5 the doubled pawns hinder White's attacking operations and his only chance consists then in the maneuver Ng4-f6 +, but this is far in the future.

21...Nxg5

Not 21...Nxd4 due to 22.Qf2.

22.hxg5 Rd8 23.Ng4 Ng6

Still not being able to make up his mind to play ...Bd7. It was better to keep the g6 square free for his Queen. The text weakens his f7 and gives White a tempo for doubling his Rooks on the h-file.

24.Kg2

A common move in these positions that prepares to bring the major pieces over to the h-file. Black is now without a defense.

24...Bd7 25.Bxd7 Rxd7 26.Rh1 Qe6

If 26...Nf8, then 27.Nf6 + gxf6 28.gxf6 Bd8 29.Qg4 + Ng6 30.Qh5 Nf8 31.Qh6 winning.

27.Rh5 Rb6 28.Rah1 Nf8

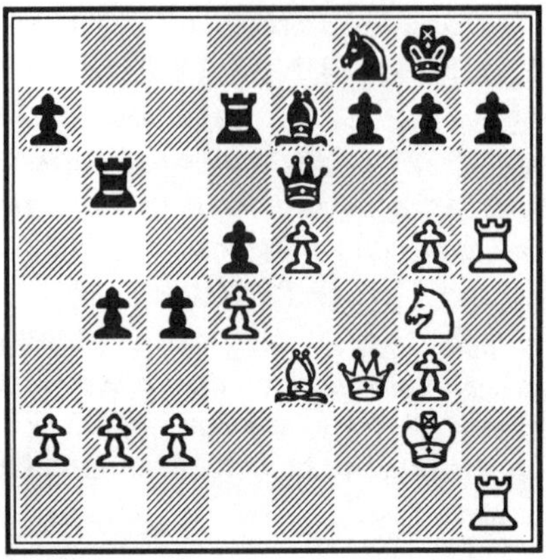

29.Nf6+

The quickest way to win.

29...gxf6 30.gxf6 Bxf6

Black must return the piece. If 30...Bd8, then 31.Rg5+ Ng6 32.Qh5.

31.exf6 Qe4

The ending will be lost as Black's pawns are weak and fall one after another. However, after 31...Qxf6 32.Rf5 (Panov's recommendation 32.Qg4+ gets nowhere after 32...Qg7) 32...Qe6 33.R1h5 Qe4 34.Qxe4 dxe4 35.Rc5 the position is reduced to much the same situation as in the game.

32.Qxe4 dxe4 33.Rg5+ Ng6 34.Rc5

Threatening 35.Rc8+ Nf8 36.Bh6.

34...Rxf6 35.Rc8+ Nf8 36.Rh4

This is much simpler than 36.Bh6 Rxh6 37.Rxh6 Rxd4.

36...Kg7 37.Rxe4 Ra6 38.Rxc4 Rb7 39.d5 Rxa2 40.Rxb4 Rxb2

A blunder, losing a Rook in a hopeless position.

41.Bd4+ 1-0

Illustrative Game 27

GM Tigran Petrosian

IM Ilya Kan

USSR Championship 1955

1.e4 c5 2.Nf3 e6 3.d3 d5 4.Nbd2

Not 4.g3 dxe4 5.dxe4 Qxd1+ and White has nothing.

4...Nc6 5.g3 Nf6 6.Bg2 Be7 7.O-O O-O 8.Re1 dxe4

Better is 8...b5.

9.dxe4 b6 10.e5 Nd7

Better is 10...Nd5, according to Levenfish.

11.Ne4

According to Levenfish, White wins material after 11.Nd4 cxd4 12.Bxc6 Rb8 13.Nb3 Qc7 14.Nxd4 Nxe5 15.Rxe5 Qxe5 16.Bf4 Qc5 17.Bxb8 Rd8 18.c3 e5 19.Bc7 Rf8 20.Qa4 exd4 21.cxd4 Qh5 22.Qxa7.

11...Ba6 12.Bf4 b5 13.c3 Qb6

Better is 13...Nb6 followed by 14...Nd5.

14.Qc2

Of course not 14.Qxd7 Rfd8.

14...Rfd8

Making room for the Knight on f8 for defensive purposes.

15.h4 Nf8 16.h5 Rac8

Better is 16...h6 to stop White's next move.

17.h6 Ng6

Worse is 17...g6 18.Bg5.

18.hxg7 Kxg7

If 18...Nxf4, then 19.gxf4 Kxg7 20.Kh2 planning Bh3 followed by f4-f5.

19.Qc1 Rd3 20.Bg5

Exchanging Bishops leaves Black very weak on the dark squares.

20...Bxg5

If 20...Qd8, then 21.Bf6+ Kg8 22.Nxc5.

21.Qxg5 Rxf3

A futile Exchange sacrifice which hardly slows White's attack.

22.Bxf3 Nxe5 23.Qf6+ Kg8 24.Rad1 Bb7 25.Bh5 Bd5 26.Qg5 Nd7 27.Bxg6 hxg6 28.Qe7 Rc7

29.Qh4

Question 11: Why doesn't White play 29.Nd6?

29...Rc8

If 29...Bxa2, then 30.Rxd7.

30.b3 Kg7 31.Qe7 Nf8

31...Qd8 would have held out longer.

32.Nd6 1-0

Illustrative Game 28

GM Bobby Fischer
NM Lhamsuren Miagmasuren

Sousse 1967

1.e4 e6 2.d3 d5 3.Nd2 Nf6 4.g3 c5 5.Bg2 Nc6 6.Ngf3 Be7 7.O-O O-O 8.e5 Nd7 9.Re1 b5 10.Nf1 b4 11.h4 a5 12.Bf4 a4 13.a3

A new idea at the time. Before continuing with his kingside attack, White takes defensive measures on the queenside. ...a4-a3 is prevented, which would have created a hole at c3.

13...bxa3 14.bxa3 Na5

Placing the Knight on the rim is dubious. Better is 15...Ba6.

15.Ne3 Ba6 16.Bh3

Preventing Black from playing ...f6 or ...f5.

16...d4

Gaining the d5 square, but giving up the e4 square, which will later play a decisive role in White's attack.

17.Nf1 Nb6 18.Ng5 Nd5

Perhaps better is 18...h6 19.Ne4 c4.

19.Bd2 Bxg5

Now 19...h6 is impossible due to 20.Nxe6 fxe6 21.Bxe6+ Kh8 22.Bxa5 Qxa5 23.Bxd5.

20.Bxg5 Qd7 21.Qh5 Rfc8 22.Nd2

More pieces are coming to the kingside for the decisive attack.

22...Nc3

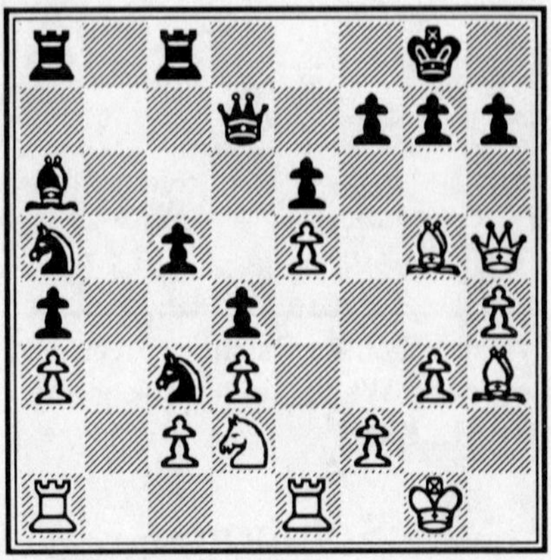

23.Bf6!

Threatening 24.Qg5 g6 25.Qh6. The Bishop is immune because of 23...gxf6 24.exf6 Kh8 25.Nf3 Nd5 (25...Rg8 26.Ne5) 26.Ng5 Nxf6 27.Qh6 Qe7 28.Bf5 Rg8 29.Nxh7 winning.

23...Qe8 24.Ne4

White will exchange the Knight on c3 in order to bring the Rook to the kingside via e4. 25.Nd6 is threatened.

24...g6 25.Qg5 Nxe4 26.Rxe4 c4

Black's queenside counterplay is too slow.

27.h5 cxd3 28.Rh4 Ra7

If 28...dxc2, then 29.hxg6 c1=Q+ 30.Rxc1 Rxc1+ 31.Kh2 fxg6 32.Rxh7 Kxh7 33.Qh4+ Kg8 34.Qh8+ Kf7 35.Qg7 mate. The text move counters this threat by guarding h7.

29.Bg2!

The Bishop enters the attack by repositioning on the e4 square.

29...dxc2

If 29...Qf8, then 30.Be4 dxc2 (30...h6 31.hxg6) 31.hxg6 fxg6 32.Bxg6 hxg6 33.Rh8+ Kf7 34.Rh7+ Ke8 35.Rxa7 winning.

30.Qh6 Qf8 31.Qxh7+! 1-0

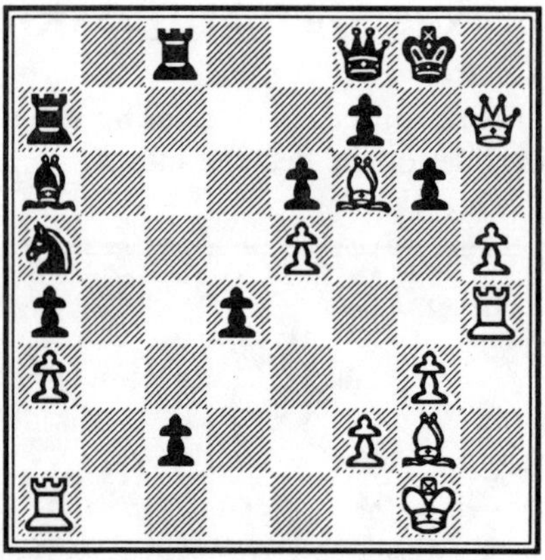

A spectacular finish! **Question 12: How does White finish the game off after 31...Kxh7**

Solutions:

Question 1: 31.g7 wins immediately.

Question 2: 34.Nf6+ Ke7 35.Rb7+.

Question 3: Because of 14.f4 winning a piece.

Question 4: 32.Nxe6 fxe6 33.Rxe4.

Question 5: 27...d4 28.Bd2 c4 was faster.

Question 6: Due to 25...Be7.

Question 7: 30.Rxg7 Qxg7 31.Qxc6+.

Question 8: 32.Qf8+ Kh7 33.Qxd8 Qxb3 34.Qxe7.

Question 9: 29...Rg1+ mating.

Question 10: 30.Re8+ Qxe8 31.Qxh7+ Kf8 32.g7+ and 33.g8=Q+.

Question 11: Because of 29...Nf8.

Question 12: 32.hxg6+ Kxg6 33.Be4 mate.

A Defense to 1.d4: The King's Indian Defense

If you liked the King's Indian Attack for White because of the dangerous attacks you can get, then you will also want to play it with Black. Black can play a King's Indian set-up to any White reply execpt 1.e4. As in the previous chapter, his first moves usually consist of 1...Nf6, 2...g6, 3...Bg7, 4...d6 and 5...O-O. Again, his plan will be to play ...e7-e5.

White plays a classical set-up

The classical set-up results after 1.d4 Nf6 2.c4 g6 3.Nc3 Bg7 4.e4 d6 5.Nf3 O-O 6.Be2 e5 7.O-O Nc6 8.d5 Ne7 and now Black's plan is to move his King Knight out of the way so that he can advance his f-pawn and start a kingside attack.

Illustrative Game 1

GM Svetozar Gligoric

GM Robert Fischer

Bled 1961

1.d4 Nf6 2.c4 g6 3.Nc3 Bg7 4.e4 d6 5.Nf3 O-O 6.Be2 e5 7.O-O

White cannot win a pawn with 7.dxe5 dxe5 8.Qxd8 Rxd8 9.Nxe5 due to 9...Nxe4.

7...Nc6 8.d5 Ne7 9.Ne1 Nd7 10.Nd3 f5 11.exf5

Otherwise Black plays 11...f4, starting a kingside attack.

11...Nxf5

This Knight will find a strong outpost at d4, but White gets a grip on the e4-square. An alternative is 11...exf5.

12.f3 Nf6 13.Nf2 Nd4 14.N2e4 Nh5 15.Bg5 Qd7

This move looks awkward, but Fischer has seen far ahead.

16.g3 h6 17.Be3 c5!

Gligoric thought that Fischer was dropping a pawn with this move.

18.Bxd4 exd4 19.Nb5 a6 20.Nbxd6 d3! 21.Qxd3 Bd4+ 22.Kg2

22...Nxg3!

This is the move that Fischer visualized when playing his 17th move.

23.Nxc8!

Not 24.hxg3 Qh3#. If 24.Nxg3, then 24...Qxd6 is good for Black.

23...Nxf1 24.Nb6! Qc7

Threatening mate on h2.

25.Rxf1 Qxb6

Black has won the Exchange, but White starts a very strong counterattack.

26.b4! Qxb4

26...cxb4 27.c5 is good for White. For example, if 27...Bxc5, then 28.Nxc5 Qxc5 29.Qxg6+ Kh8 30.Qxh6+ Kg8 31.Kh1 wins.

27.Rb1 Qa5

Question 1: How does Black defend if White plays 28.Rxb7?

28.Nxc5 Qxc5 29.Qxg6+ Bg7 30.Rxb7 Qd4

The only defense.

31.Bd3 Rf4 32.Qe6+ Kh8 33.Qg6 Draw

Illustrative Game 2

GM Mark Taimanov
GM Miguel Najdorf

Zurich 1953

1.d4 Nf6 2.c4 g6 3.Nc3 Bg7 4.e4 d6 5.Nf3 O-O 6.Be2 e5 7.O-O Nc6 8.d5 Ne7 9.Ne1 Nd7

With this pawn structure, White plays for the c4-c5 break and Black for the f7-f5 break.

10.Be3 f5 11. f3 f4 12.Bf2 g5 13.Nd3 Nf6 14.c5

With the center closed, each side attacks on the flank.

14...Ng6 15.Rc1 Rf7 16.Rc2 Bf8

Defending the d-pawn and allowing the Rook to get to the g-file.

17.cxd6 cxd6 18.Qd2 g4 19.Rfc1

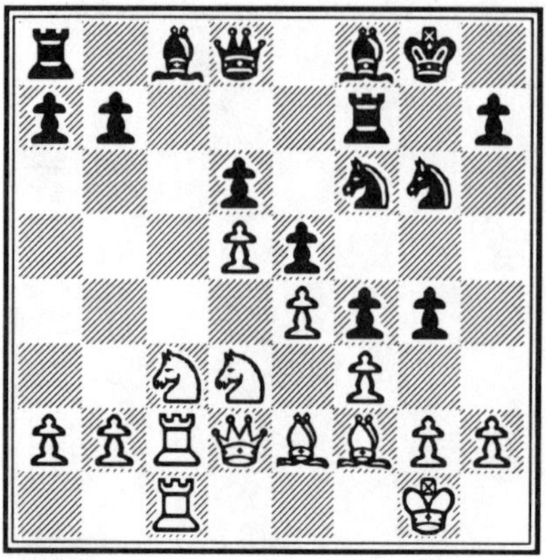

19...g3!

Sacrificing a pawn to open up the kingside.

20.hxg3 fxg3 21.Bxg3 Nh5 22.Bh2 Be7 23.Nb1 Bd7 24.Qe1 Bg5 25.Nd2 Be3+ 26.Kh1 Qg5 27.Bf1

27.Nc4, sacrificing the Exchange, offered better chances.

27...Raf8 28.Rd1 b5 29.a4 a6 30.axb5 axb5 31.Rc7 Rg7 32.Nb3 Nh4 33.Rc2 Bh3

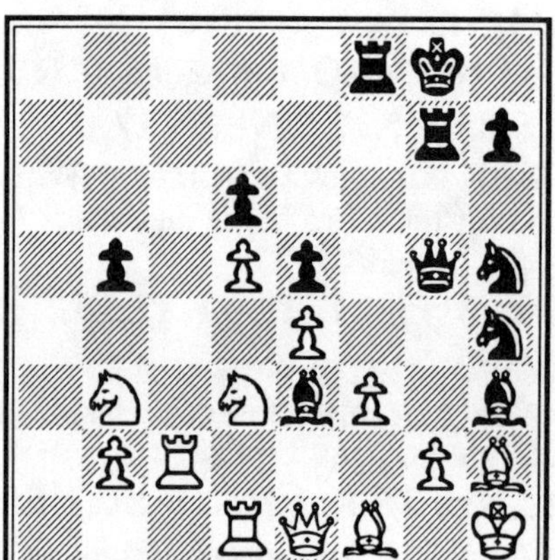

Threatening 34...Rxf3.

34.Qe2

Question 2: How does Black reply to 34.gxh3?

34...Nxg2 35.Bxg2 Bxg2+ 36.Qxg2 Qh4 37.Qxg7+

If 37.Qe2, then 37...Ng3+.

37...Kxg7 38.Rg2+ Kh8 39.Ne1 Nf4 40.Rg3 Bf2 41.Rg4 Qh3 42.Nd2 h5 0-1

If 43.Rg5, then 43...Rg8 44.Rxg8+ Kxg8 leads to mate.

Illustrative Game 3

GM Tigran Petrosian
GM Svetozar Gligoric

Yugoslavia 1970

1.c4 g6 2.Nf3 Bg7 3.d4 Nf6 4.Nc3 O-O 5.e4 d6 6.Be2 e5 7.O-O Nc6 8.d5 Ne7 9.b4 Nh5 10.Nd2 Nf4 11.a4 f5 12.Bf3 g5! 13.exf5 Nxf5 14.g3

If 14.Nde4, then 14...Nh4 is strong.

14...Nd4 15.gxf4 Nxf3+

Even stronger is 15...exf4!

16.Qxf3 g4 17.Qh1

17.Qd3 offered more chances.

17...exf4 18.Bb2 Bf5 19.Rfe1 f3 20.Nde4 Qh4 21.h3 Be5 22.Re3

If 22.hxg4, then 22...Qxg4+ 23.Kf1 Bxc3.

22...gxh3 23.Qxf3 Bg4 24.Qh1 h2+ 25.Kg2

If 25.Kf1, then 25...Rf3!

25...Qh5 26.Nd2 Bd4!

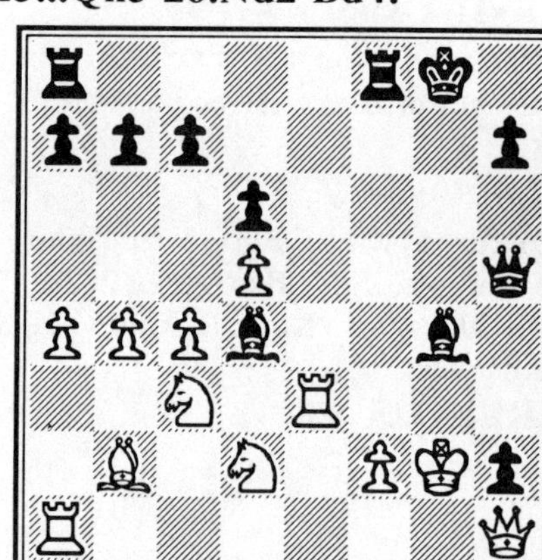

Question 3: How would Black finish off White after 27.Rae1?

27.Qe1 Rae8 28.Nce4

If 28.Nd1, then 28...Rxe3 29.fxe3 Bxb2 30.Nxb2 Bh3+ 31.Kxh2 Bf1+

32.Kg1 Qg4+ wins.

28...Bxb2 29.Rg3 Be5! 30.Raa3 Kh8 31.Kh1 Rg8 32.Qf1 Bxg3 33.Rxg3? Rxe4 0-1

Illustrative Game 4

GM Bent Larsen

GM Mikhail Tal

Match 1969

1.Nf3 Nf6 2.c4 g6 3.Nc3 Bg7 4.e4 d6 5.d4 O-O 6.Be2 e5 7.O-O Nc6 8.d5 Ne7 9.Ne1 Nd7 10.Nd3 f5 11.Bd2 Nf6 12.f3 f4 13.c5 g5 14.Rc1 Ng6 15.Nb5 Rf7 16.cxd6 cxd6 17.Qc2 g4 18.Nc7 gxf3 19.gxf3 Bh3 20.Nxa8 Nxe4 21.fxe4 Qg5+ 22.Kf2 Qg2+

The game Adamski–Geller, Budapest 1970 ended in a draw after 22...Qh4+ 23.Kg1 Qg5+ 24.Kf2.

23.Ke1 Nh4 24.Be3?

Better is 24.Nf2 Nf3+ 25.Kd1 Nd4 26.Qc3.

24...Qxe4! 25.Bf2 f3 26.Bxh4

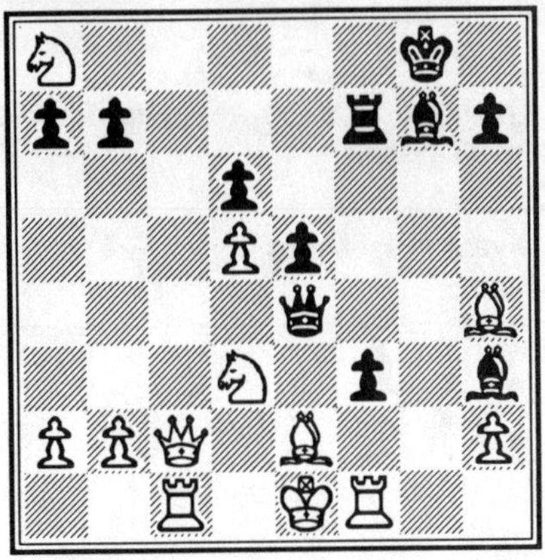

Question 4: On 26...Bxf1, should White play 27.Kxf1?

26...Qxh4+ 27.Nf2 fxe2 28.Qxe2 e4! 29.Rg1

If 29.Rc7, then 29...Bxf1 30.Kxf1 Rf5 is strong.

29...e3 30.Qxe3 Re7 31.Rxg7+ Kxg7 32.Rc7 Bd7 33.Rxd7 Rxd7 34.Qxa7?

White had drawing chances with 34.Qc3+ Qf6 35.Qg3+! Kf8 36.Nd3.

34...Re7+ 35.Kd1

35.Kf1 offered better chances.

35...Qc4 36.Qb6 Qf1+ 37.Kd2 Re2+ 38.Kc3 Qc1+ 39.Kd4 Qe3+ 40.Kc4 Rc2+ 0-1

Xie Jun has been called the female Kasparov, witness here her handling of the King's Indian Defense. This was the big difference in the match in her 1993 women's world championship match against Nona Ioseliani, with Xie Jun scoring 5.5-0.5 with the KID. Much of Ioseliani's difficulties in the match were caused by severe time pressure, beginning with the first game.

Illustrative Game 5

WGM Nana Ioseliani

WGM Xie Jun

Monaco (1) 1993

1.d4 Nf6 2.c4 g6 3.Nc3 Bg7 4.e4 d6 5.Be2 O-O 6.Nf3 e5 7.Be3 h6 8.O-O Ng4 9.Bc1 Nc6 10.d5 Ne7 11.Ne1 h5

11...f5 is more common.

12.h3

Poluljahov–Rechel, Anapa 1991, continued 12.f3 Nh6 13.Nd3 f5 14.f4 Nf7 15.fxe5 Nxe5 16.Nxe5 Bxe5 17.Bh6 Rf7 18.Qd2 fxe4 19.Qg5?! Bf5 20.h3 Bf6 with a very good position for Black.

12...Nh6 13.Nd3 f5 14.f4 Nf7 15.fxe5 dxe5?!

This keeps a fluid pawn center, but later Black will have to worry about c4-c5. 15...Nxe5 was worth considering, as in the game given above.

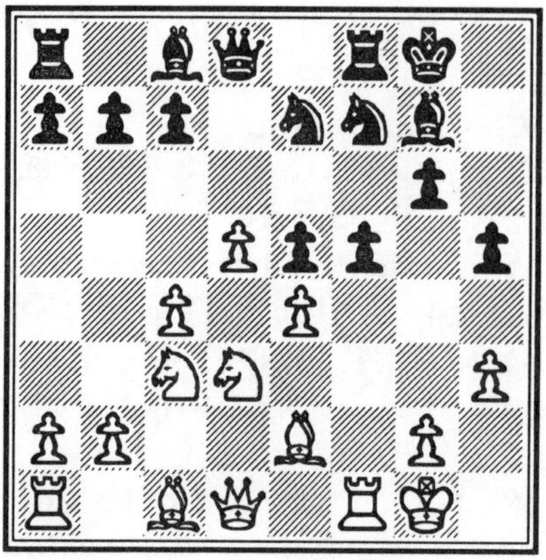

16.Nc5

This loses time, as the Knight shortly returns to d3. Perhaps she was hoping to play 17.Ne6. An immediate 16.b4 or 16.c5 fxe4 17.Nf2 was worth considering. Black still manages to get into a difficult position.

16...f4

Now 17.Ne6 can be met with 17...Bxe6 18.dxe6 Ng5.

17.b4 Ng5 18.Kh2

An immediate sacrifice on h3 does not look sound. However, this could be possible later on, so White strengthens her defenses.

18...Kh8

The Knight on e7 is terribly placed. Therefore, it will move to a better square via g8.

19.Nd3 Ng8 20.Bb2 Qe7

To protect the e-pawn.

21.c5 Nf6 22.Nf2

White is threatening to crash through in the center with d5-d6 and the Women's World Champion did not want to defend passively with ...Rf8-d8. Before she starts action on the kingside, she disorganizes White's pieces on the queenside, which could be useful in the tactics that follow.

22...a5 23.Ba3

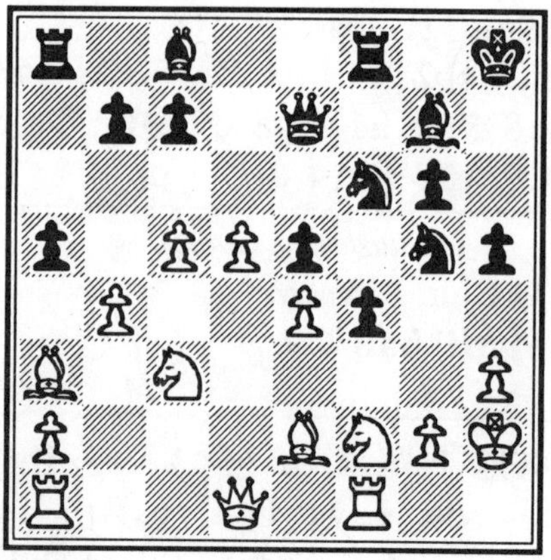

23...f3

Sacrificing a pawn to open lines.

24.gxf3

Not 24.Bxf3 Nxf3+ 25.gxf3 Nh7 which is very good for Black.

24...Nfh7

Threatening 25...Nxh3 26.Nxh3 Qh4.

25.Kg2

With White threatening 26.d6, Black must continue sacrificing to keep the attack going.

25...Nxh3?!

This is unsound, although her position seems to be inferior and an alternative is hard to find.

26.Nxh3 Ng5 27.Ng1

Question 5: What happens if White plays 27.Nxg5?

27...Ne6

Again, Black has no choice but to sacrifice.

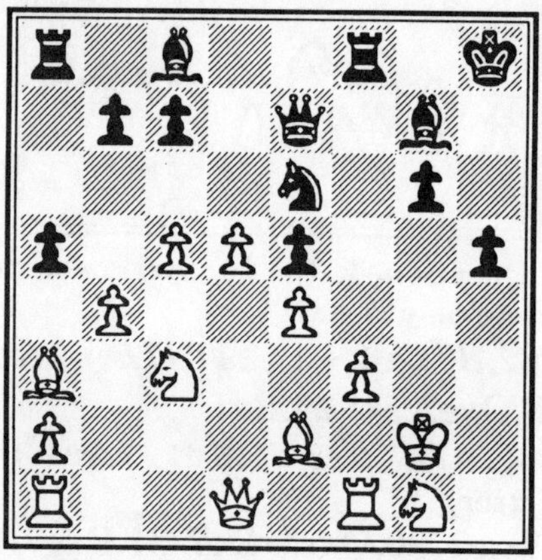

28.Rf2

Despite being short on time, Ioseliani finds the best move. 28.dxe6?! allows Black a perpetual check after 28...axb4 29.Bxb4 Qg5+ 30.Kf2 (or 30.Kh2 Qh4+) 30...Qh4+, since 31.Kg2 is forced, as 31.Ke3? leads to a decisive attack for Black after 31...Bh6+ 32.Kd3 Rd8+ 33.Nd5 (33.Kc2 Rxd1 34.Raxd1 Bxe6) 33...Rxd5+ 34.exd5 Qxb4.

28...Nf4+ 29.Kf1??

A very unfortunate move. The King is safe after 29.Kh1 and White wins.

29...Qh4

The White King cannot escape: 30.Ke1 Ng2+.

30.b5?

White falls apart in time pressure. She should try to hold with 30.Bc4 and if 30...Qh1, then 31.Ne2.

30...Qh1

Crushing. Black threatens 31...Bh3+.

31.Ke1 Qxg1+ 32.Rf1 Ng2+ 33.Kd2 Qd4+ 34.Bd3 Bh6+ 0-1

Illustrative Game 6

WGM Nana Ioseliani

WGM Xie Jun

Monaco (5) 1993

1.d4 Nf6 2.c4 g6 3.Nc3 Bg7 4.e4 d6 5.Be2 O-O 6.Nf3 e5 7.O-O Nc6 8.d5 Ne7 9.Nd2 a5 10.a3 Bd7 11.Rb1 a4 12.b4 axb3 13.Nxb3 b6

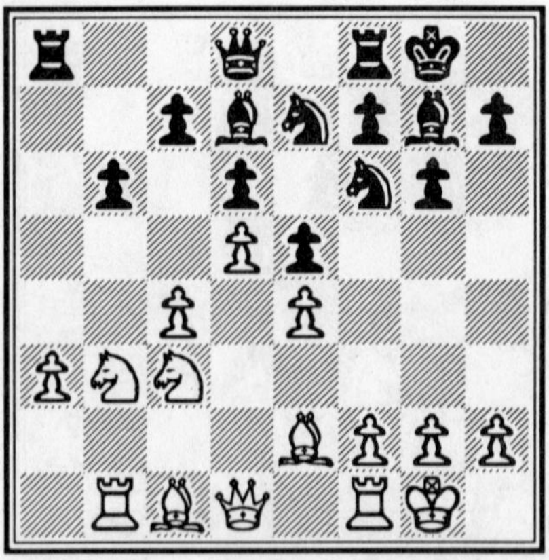

White's usual plan in this opening is to break with c4-c5. Black has taken time to prevent this with her last few moves. She wants to slow down White's queenside attack before starting her own attack. If Black is given too much time, her coming attack on the kingside will be unstoppable. Therefore, White must quickly break through on the queenside. This can only be accomplished by advancing the a-pawn: Ra1, a3-a4-a5. Black will then have to play ...bxa5, losing her stranglehold of the c5-square and then White will be able to play c4-c5.

14.Ra1 Ne8

In the game Chabanon–Kr. Georgiev, Sofia 1990, Black tried to delay White's advance of the a-pawn with 14...Qe8, but after 15.Qd3 Ba4 16.Bd1 Kh8 17.Be3 Neg8 18.Nxa4 Rxa4 19.Nd2 Ra5 20.c5! bxc5 21.Nc4 Ra7 22.a4 White had a winning position.

15.Be3 f5 16.f3 Kh8 17.a4

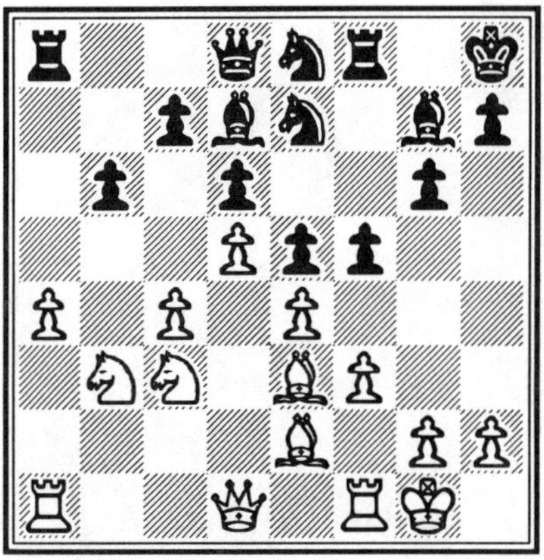

17...c5

Lputian–Kupreichik, Minsk 1987, continued 17...Ng8 18.a5 bxa5 19.Nxa5 Bh6 20.Bxh6 Nxh6 21.Qd2 Nf7 22.c5 dxc5 23.Nb7 Qb8 24.Nxc5 with a very good position for White. The text appears to be a strategically powerful move and makes a White breakthrough on the queenside much less effective.

18.Ra2

18.dxc6 Bxc6 is fine for Black.

18...Nf6 19.Qa1 f4 20.Bf2 g5 21.Nb5 Bxb5 22.cxb5

Now White threatens to play 23.a5, opening the a-file and creating a passed b-pawn. However, White's attack has been slow and Black is already knocking at the door on the kingside.

22...g4 23.a5

Perhaps because of Black's next move, 23.Bh4 should have been played.

23...g3

This move often leads to a very strong attack in such positions. White has no choice but to allow lines to start getting opened up.

24.hxg3 Nh5 25.axb6 Rxa2 26.Qxa2 fxg3 27.b7

White must sacrifice the Bishop and bank her hopes on the passed b-pawn: 27.Be3 Ng6 followed by 28...Qh4 wins immediately for Black.

27...Ng6 28.Bc4 Qh4 29.Ra1 gxf2+ 30.Qxf2 Ng3 31.Qe1 Qh1+ 32.Kf2 Qh4 33.Kg1

White is very short on time and is happy to repeat moves. But if 33.Ke3, then 33...Bh6+ 34.Kd3 Nf4+ 35.Kc2 Nxg2 36.Qc3 Ne3+ is killing. Or if 33.Ra8, then 33...Nf4 (less clear is 33...Nxe4+ 34.Ke2 Nf4+ 35.Kd1) 34.Qg1 Nge2+ 35.Kf1 Nxg1 36.Rxf8+ Bxf8 37.b8=Q Kg8 38.Kxg1 Qe1+ 39.Kh2 Qf2, winning.

33...Nf4

Question 6: What is Black threatening?

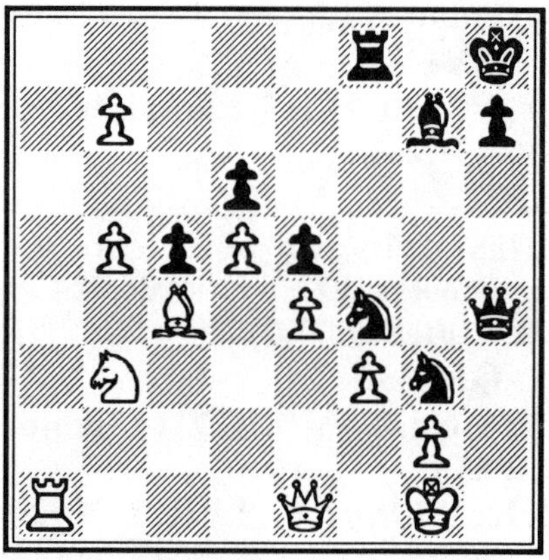

34.Bf1?

Correct is 34.Ra8 Qh1+ 35.Kf2 with an extremely complicated position. Now 35...Nh3+ looks strong, but White can actually hold a draw after 36.Kxg3! Qxe1+ 37.Kxh3. However, it is unclear that Black has anything better. For example, 35...Qxg2+ 36.Ke3 Qc2 37.Rxf8+ Bxf8 38.Qd2 is good for White. Unfortunately, as in game one, Ioseliani misses the correct defense in time pressure.

34...Bh6

Not immediately 34...Qh1+ 35.Kf2 Nh3+ 36.Ke3.

35.Ra8 Qh1+ 36.Kf2 Nh3+ 37.Kxg3

37.gxh3 Qxf3+ also leads to mate.

37...Bf4+ 38.Kg4 h5+ 0-1

39.Kxh5 Nf2+ 40.Kg6 Qh7 mate. Ioseliani has at most a minute left on her clock.

Illustrative Game 7

WGM Nana Ioseliani

WGM Xie Jun

Monaco (7) 1993

1.d4 Nf6 2.Nf3 g6 3.c4 Bg7 4.Nc3 O-O 5.e4 d6 6.Be2 e5 7.O-O Nc6 8.d5 Ne7 9.Nd2 a5 10.a3 Nd7

Deviating from 10...Bd7 as played in game five. The text move has been a favorite of Judith Polgar.

11.Rb1 f5 12.b4 Kh8 13.f3 axb4

Often this exchange is delayed in favor of 13...f4, 13...Bh6, or 13...Ng8. 13...c6 was played in game three.

14.axb4 c6

Although a common move in the KID, this appears to be a novelty in this particular position. Judith Polgar has played 14...Ng8 in many games. Khalifman–J. Polgar, Dos Hermanas 1993, continued 14...Ng8 15.Qc2 Bh6 16.c5 dxc5 17.Nb5 c6 18.dxc6 bxc6 19.Nd6 cxb4 20.exf5 Ndf6 21.Nxc8 gxf5 22.Nc4 Bxc1 23.Rfxc1 Rxc8 24.Rxb4 Qd4+ 25.Kh1 Rcd8 26.Rb7 Nh5 and Black went on to win.

15.Kh1

15.dxc6 Nxc6 16.Nb3 transposes into game three, when White got nothing.

15...Nf6 16.Nb3 cxd5 17.cxd5 f4 18.Na5 g5 19.Nc4 Ng6 20.b5 Rg8 21.Bd2 Bf8 22.Re1 h5 23.Ra1 Rb8 24.Na4 g4 25.Nab6 g3

As in the fifth game, Black starts creating dangerous mating threats after this move.

26.Nxc8

White must exchange off this Bishop to prevent Black from sacrificing it on h3 after h2-h3 is played.

26...Rxc8 27.Ba5 Qe7 28.h3 Nh7

Black begins to reposition her Knights in preparation for a sacrifice on h3.

29.Qd3 Ng5 30.Rg1 Nh4 31.Nb6?

Once again, short on time, Ioseliani misplays the defense. It is hard to see how Black could immediately breakthrough after 31.Bf1. Now Xie Jun has a forced win.

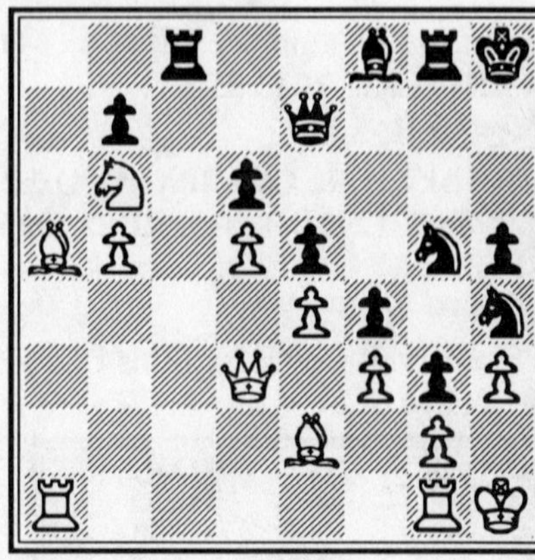

Black to play and win.

31...Nxh3!

Of course there is no time for 32.Nxc8 due to 32...Nf2 mate.

32.gxh3 g2+ 33.Rxg2

Question 7: What should Black play against 33.Kh2?

33...Nxg2 34.Rg1

White cannot survive long after 34.Nxc8 Qh4.

34...Rc1!

The key move in the combination. Sacrificing the Rook gives Black's Queen time to decisively invade the kingside.

35.Rxc1 Qh4 36.Bf1 Qxh3+ 37.Kg1 Ne1+ 38.Kf2 Qg3+ 39.Ke2 Nxd3 40.Kxd3 Qxf3+ 41.Kc2 0-1

Illustrative Game 8

WGM Nana Ioseliani
WGM Xie Jun

Monaco (9) 1993

1.d4 Nf6 2.c4 g6 3.Nc3 Bg7 4.e4 d6 5.Nf3 O-O 6.Be2 e5 7.Be3 c6

Deviating from game one, which continued 7...h6.

8.d5

Black would equalize after 8.O-O exd4 9.Nxd4 Re8 10.f3 d5.

8...Ng4 9.Bg5 f6

Too risky is 9...Qb6 10.O-O Qxb2 11.Na4 Qa3 12.Bc1 Qb4 13.Bd2 Qa3 14.Rb1.

10.Bh4

White has also retreated this Bishop back to c1 or d2.

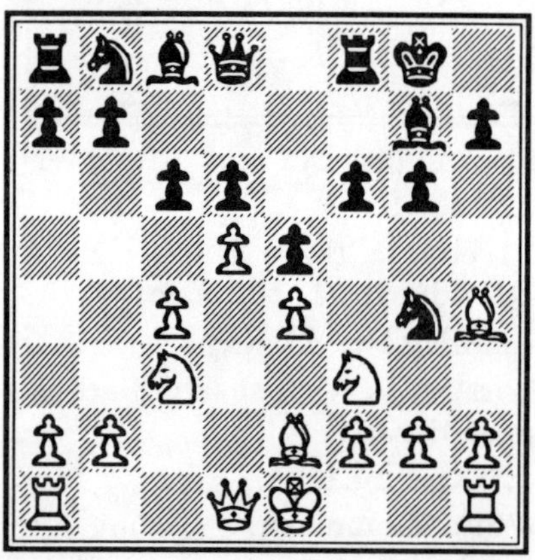

10...h5

The usual move has been 10...Na6. The 19th game of the Karpov–Kasparov New York/Lyons match continued 11.Nd2 Nh6 12.a3 Nf7 13.f3 Bh6. Later Kasparov offered a draw in a much better position. In her game with Maric in the 1991 Candidates match in Beijing, Xie Jun played 13...c5 14.Rb1 Bd7 and a draw was agreed to ten moves later.

11.Nd2 Nh6 12.f3 c5 13.O-O Nf7 14.Bd3 Bh6 15.Qe2 Na6 16.a3

Black has a fine position. White's only break is b2-b4, but this is unlikely to cause Black any problems.

16...Bg5 17.Bxg5

Exchanging off Black's bad Bishop and giving her the ...g5-g4 break. But Black looks good after 17.Bf2 f5.

17...fxg5 18.Qe3 Bd7 19.Rab1 Qe7 20.b4 Nd8 21.Bc2 b6 22.Ba4

Exchanging off her bad Bishop.

22...Bxa4 23.Nxa4 Nb7 24.Nc3 Kg7 25.Nb5 Rfc8 26.Kh1 Nc7 27.Nc3 Rf8 28.Ne2 Na6 29.g3 Nd8 30.b5

White gets nothing with 30.bxc5. So instead she plays for the a4-a5 break.

31...Nc7 31.a4 Nf7 32.a5 Ne8 33.Ra1 Nf6 34.Ra3 Rab8 35.Rfa1 Rb7 36.Rf1 Rbb8 37.Nc3 g4 38.f4 exf4 39.gxf4 h4 40.Qe2

White's play has been very lack-luster, but at least she's survived the time control this time.

40...g3 41.h3 Nh5 42.Nd1 Nh6

Question 8: Is 42...g2+ a good move?

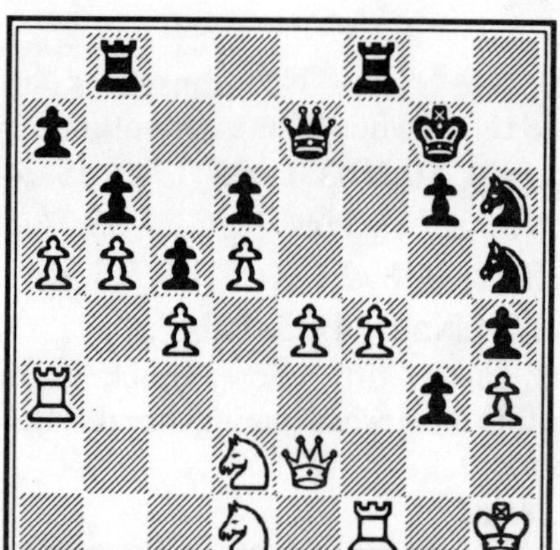

43.Raf3?

This terrible move allows Black to get her Knight to d4 and Ioseliani's position quickly falls apart. It is very hard to understand this move, because she could not have been in time trouble at this point. Correct is 43.Qe3.

43...Nf5 44.e5 Nd4 45.Qe4 g2+ 46.Kxg2 Nxf3 47.Rxf3 Nxf4+ 48.Kh2 Qg5 49.Ne3 Ne2 50.Qg4 Qxe5+ 0-1

Illustrative Game 9

WGM Nana Ioseliani

WGM Xie Jun

Monaco (11) 1993

1.d4 Nf6 2.c4 g6 3.Nc3 Bg7 4.e4 d6 5.Nf3 O-O 6.Be2 e5 7.Be3 c6 8.d5 Ng4 9.Bg5 f6 10.Bh4 h5 11.Nd2 Na6

Deviating from 11...Nh6, as played in game nine.

12.a3 Nh6 13.f3 Nf7 14.dxc6

White wants a different type of pawn formation than in game nine, which would reappear after 14.b4 c5. In that game White achieved nothing.

14...bxc6 15.b4 Nc7 16.Nb3 Ne6 17.O-O Nf4 18.Re1 Be6 19.Bf1 g5 20.Bf2 f5 21.Na5 Qd7 22.c5?

This gives up much of the center. Better is 22.b5

22...d5

A very complex situation, beginning with a sacrifice, is about to occur. Xie Jun has excelled throughout the match in these tactical situations.

23.g3

Now one might expect 23...d4 or 23...Ng6. But, as usual, Xie Jun has different ideas.

23...fxe4! 24.fxe4

Ioseliani does not seem to want to accept the sacrifice, perhaps because of her bad experiences in the previous games. But 24.gxf4 exf4 25.fxe4 d4 would transpose to the actual game in any case.

24...d4 25.gxf4 exf4

Xie Jun is interested in attacking, not material gain. 25...dxc3 26.f5 is good for White. Now Black's attack looks extremely dangerous. In addition to the advancing kingside pawns, her Knight has a beautiful square on e5.

26.Nxc6?!

White sacrifices back the piece to try to slow the attack by forcing a Queen exchange, but to no avail. However, Black's initiative after 26.Na4 Ne5 would be ferocious.

26...dxc3 27.Qxd7 Bxd7 28.Ne7+

White is too short on time to construct a credible defense, if one exists at all. Perhaps 28.Nd4 Ne5 29.b5 is worth trying.

28...Kh7 29.Rac1 g4 30.Red1 Be6 31.Nd5 Ng5 32.Nxc3 h4 33.Rd3 g3 34. Be1 Be5

Preparing to advance the f-pawn.

35.Bd2 Nh3+ 36.Kg2

If 36.Bxh3, then 36...Bxh3 37.Rd5 f3.

36...Rad8

To gain control of the f3-square.

37.Nd5

Not a fun position to play in time pressure.

Question 9: What happens if White plays 37.Rxd8

37...Bg4 0-1

White resigns with less than a minute left on her clock. Not an unfamiliar sight in this match.

The Four Pawns Attack

Usually Black's plan is to play ...e7-e5, but against the four pawns attack ...c7-c5 is better.

Illustrative Game 10

GM Wolfgang Uhlmann

GM Efim Geller

Dresden 1959

1.d4 Nf6 2.c4 d6 3.Nc3 g6 4.e4 Bg7 5.f4 c5 6.Nf3 cxd4 7.Nxd4 Nc6 8.Be2 O-O 9.Be3 Bg4 10.Nf3 e5!

Opening up the position.

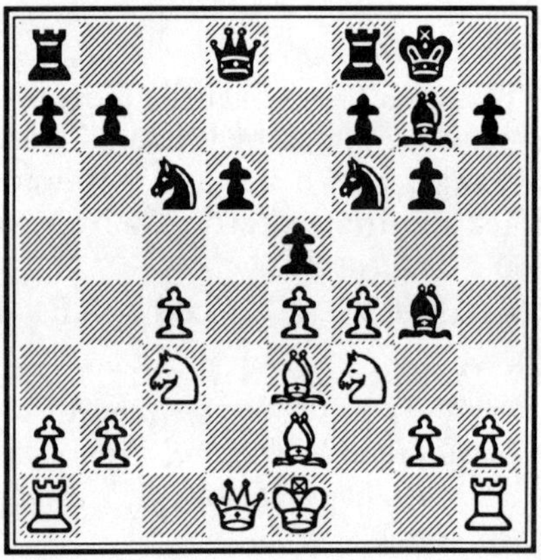

11.fxe5

Otherwise Black will open the diagonal for his King Bishop.

11...dxe5 12.O-O Qa5 13.Qe1 Rad8 14.Qh4

White is planning a kingside attack with Bh6 and Ng5. Therefore Black counterattacks in the center.

14...Nd4 15.Bg5

If 15.Ng5, then White's attack is stopped after 15...Nxe2+ 16.Nxe2 Bxe2 17.Rxf6 h6.

15...Bxf3 16.Bxf3 Qb6 17.Rf2

If 17.Kh1, then Black wins a pawn and stops White's attack after 17...Qxb2 18.Nb5 Nxb5 19.axb5 Rd6.

17...Nxf3+ 18.gxf3 Rd3

Threatening 19...Rxf3 and 19...Rc8.

19.c5 Qe6 20.Rc1 Rc8 21.Nb5 Nh5

Black has a big advantage because he controls the d-file and White's King is exposed.

22.Nxa7 Ra8 23.Nb5 h6 24.Bd2 Rxa2 25.Nc7 Qb3 26.Bc3 Nf4

Threatening 27...Rd1+ 28.Rxd1 Qxd1+ 29.Rf1 Qe2.

27.Nd5 Nxd5 28.exd5 Rxd5 29.Qb4 Qxb4 30.Bxb4 Ra4 31.Ba3 e4 32.fxe4 Rxe4 33.Kh1 Bd4 34.Rd2 Rg5 35.b4 Bc3! 36.Rd8+ Kg7 37.b5 Re2 38.h4 Rg3 39.c6 bxc6 40.bxc6 Be5

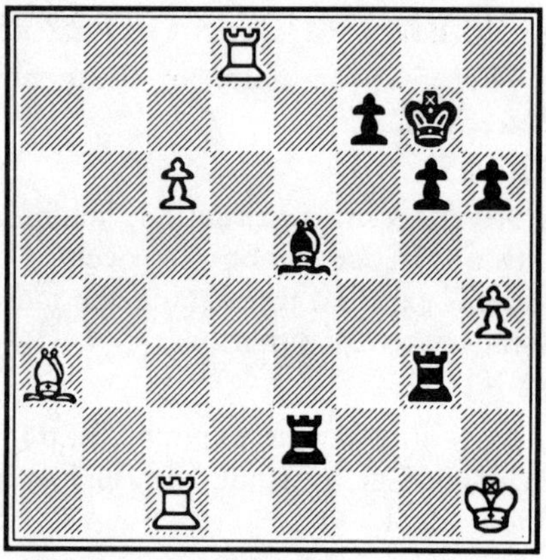

Question 10: What does Black do if White now plays 41.c7?

41.Bf8+

Here the game was adjourned but Black later resigned, as after 41...Kh7 42.c7 Rg4 43.c8=Q Rh2 it's mate.

Illustrative Game 11

GM Ivo Nei

GM Lev Polugaevsky

Tbilissi 1966/67

1.d4 Nf6 2.c4 g6 3.Nc3 Bg7 4.e4 d6 5.f4 c5 6.d5

This position was actually reached by transpostion after 1.d4 Nf6 2.c4 c5 3.d5 d6 4.Nc3 g6 5.e4 Bg7 6.f4.

6...O-O 7.Nf3 e6 8.Be2 exd5 9.e5?! Nfd7

Better is 9...Ng4 10.h3 d4 11.Ne4 Nxe5 12.fxe5 dxe5 and Black's three pawns are very strong.

10.cxd5 dxe5 11.O-O exf4 12.Bxf4 Nf6 13.Qd2 Bg4 14.h3 Bxf3 15.Bxf3 Nbd7 16.d6 Rb8 17.Rfe1 b5 18.a4 bxa4!

Opening up the position for his pieces.

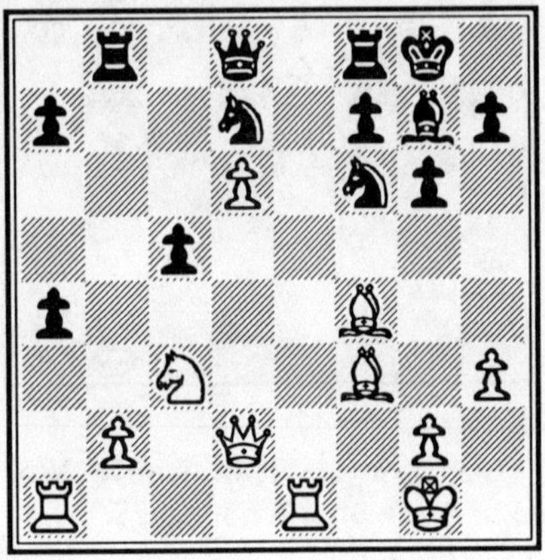

19.Rxa4 Nb6 20.Rxa7 Nc4 21.Qe2

White must give up the pawn on d6. If 21.Qf2, then 21...Nh5! threatening 22...Bd4.

21...Nxd6 22.Rd1 Nfe8 23.Be5!

Trying to exchange off Black's strong Bishop.

23...Rxb2! 24.Qe1

If 24.Qxb2, then 24...Bxe5 gives Black a very strong attack on the kingside. For example, he threatens 25...Qf6 followed by 26...Qf4.

24...Qb6 25.Bxg7

This just exchanges the active Rook on a7 for the passive one on f8. Better was 25.Rd7. If 25...Nc4, then 26.Nd5 Qe6 27.Re7 gives drawing chances.

25...Qxa7 26.Bxf8 c4+ 27.Kh1 Kxf8 28.Nd5 f6 29.Ra1 Qf7 30.Ra8 Rb5 31.Rd8

Question 11: Can Black take the Knight on d5?

31...Kg7 32.Kh2 Rc5

Threatening 33...c3 34.Nxc3 Qc7.

33.Qe3 Rxd5! 34.Bxd5 Qc7!

The White Rook cannot retreat due to 34...Nf5+.

35.Qe6 Nf5+ 36.Kh1 Qxd8 37.Qg8+ Kh6 38.g4 Nfg7 0-1

White plays a Saemisch set-up

Illustrative Game 12

GM Mikhail Tal

GM AlexanderTolush

Moscow 1957

1.c4 Nf6 2.Nc3 g6 3.e4 d6 4.d4 Bg7 5.f3 e5 6.Nge2 Nbd7 7.Bg5 c6 8.Qd2 O-O 9.d5 c5?

A strategic error. Better is 9...Nb6 10.b3 cxd5 11.cxd5 Bd7 followed by

...Rc8, creating counterplay on the queenside. Now White is able to safely castle long.

10.g4 a6 11.Ng3 Re8 12.h4 Qa5

The Queen will soon have to retreat. Better is 12...Nf8 followed by 13...Bd7.

13.Bh6 Nf8 14.h5 Qc7

Forced, as the Queen is needed in defense of the kingside after hxg6.

15.Bd3 b5 16.O-O-O

Not 16.cxb5 axb5 17.Nxb5 Qb6 followed by 18...Ba6 with counterplay on the queenside. Pawns are not important in this position, where each side is attacking the other's King. White wants to keep the queenside closed.

16...bxc4 17.Bb1!

Again White wants to keep the queenside closed. If 17.Bxc4, then ...Bd7-b5 will follow.

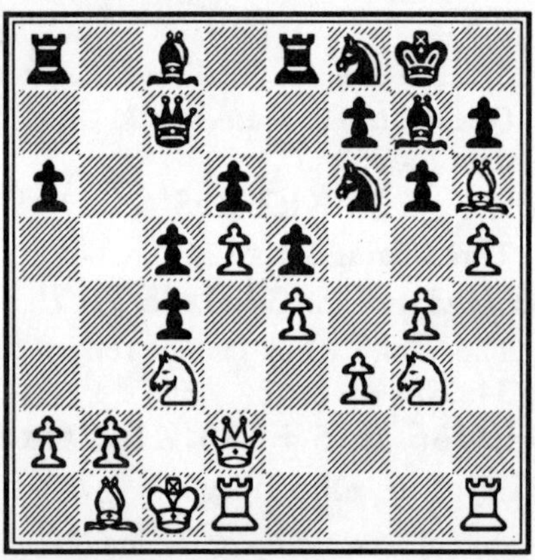

17...Bh8 18.Rdg1 Rb8 19.Nf5! N6d7 20.Bg5

Threatening 21.Ne7+ Kg7 22.h6#.

20...Bg7

If 20...f6, then 21.hxg6 hxg6 (21...fxg5 22.Qxg5) 22.Qh2 wins.

21.Nxg7 Kxg7 22.Bh6+ Kg8 23.f4!

Threatening 24.f5.

23...exf4

Now White's Bishop on b1 and Knight on c3 will come to life.

24.Qxf4 Qd8!

Not 24...Ne5? due to 25.Qf6.

25.hxg6

Black would have better defensive chances after 25.Qxd6 Rb6 26.Qf4 Ne5.

25...Nxg6 26.Qh2 Nde5 27.Bf4

White should not allow this important Bishop to be exchanged. Better is 27.Be3 Nf8 28.Qh6 Neg6 29.Bg5.

27...Nf8?

Correct is 27...Nxf4. White must play 28.Qxf4 as 28.Qh7+ Kf8 29.Qh6+ Ke7 is good for Black.

28.Qh6 Neg6

If 28...Qb6, then 29.Na4 Qa5 30.Bg5 Ned7 31.e5.

29.Bg5 f6 30.e5!

Allowing all of White's pieces to come to life.

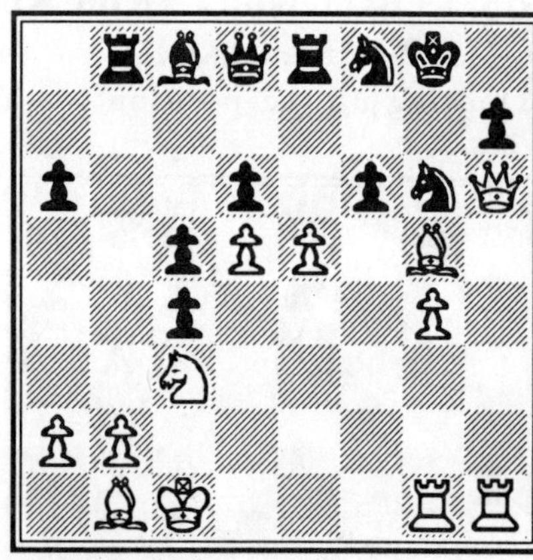

30...Rxe5

Question 12: How would White finish Black off after 30...fxg5.

31.Bxg6 Rb7

If 31...hxg6, then 32.Qh8+ Kf7 33.Rh7+ and if 31...Rxg5, then 32.Bxh7+ followed by 33.Ne4 wins.

32.Ne4! fxg5 33.Rf1

Threatening 34.Nf6+.

33...Rxe4 34.Bxe4

Threatening 35.Rxf8+ Qxf8 36.Bxh7+.

34...Rg7 35.Rf6 Bxg4 36.Rhg1 Nd7 37.Rxd6 Qe7 38.Rxa6 Kh8 39.Bxh7+! Nb8 40.Bf5+ Kg8

41.Be6+ Bxe6 42.Rxe6 1-0

Illustrative Game 13

GM Viktor Kortchnoi

GM Leonid Stein

Tallinn 1965

1.d4 Nf6 2.c4 g6 3.Nc3 Bg7 4.e4 d6 5.f3 O-O 6.Be3 e5 7.d5 Nh5 8.Qd2 f5 9.O-O-O Nd7 10.Bd3 fxe4 11.Nxe4 Nf4 12.Bc2 Nf6 13.Nc3 b5! 14.Nxb5

If 14.cxb5, then 14...a6 opens up the queenside favorably for Black.

14...Ba6 15.Na3 Rb8 16.g3 N4h5 17.b3 Bb7 18.Nb1 c6!

Opening up more lines for his pieces.

19.dxc6 Bxc6 20.Qxd6 Qe8 21.Re1 Rf7 22.Bd2 Bf8

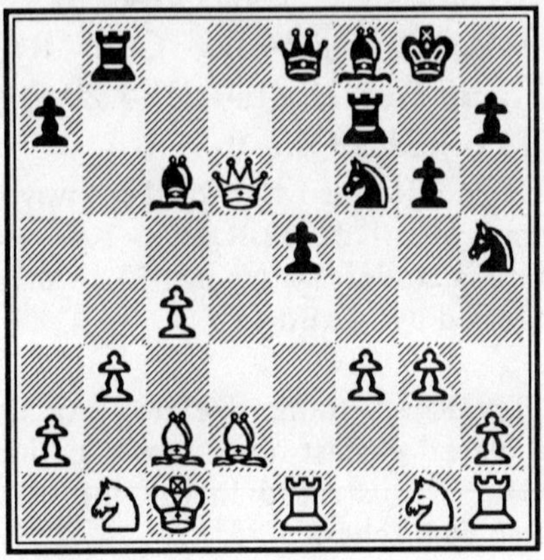

23.Qd3

Question 13: Can White take the pawn on e5 with his Queen?

23...e4! 24.Qc3

If 24.fxe4, then 24...Ng4 is strong.

24...Bg7 25.Nh3 Ng4 26.fxg4

If 26.Qxa5, then 26...Rxf3 threatening 27...e3.

26...Bxc3 27.Nxc3 Nf6 28.g5 Nd7 29.Nxe4 Qf8 30.Bc3

Hoping to play Ne4-f6+. However, 30.Nf4 offered more resistance.

30...Rf3 31.Bb2 Re8 32.Kb1

If 32.Nf4, then 32...Rxf4.

32...Bxe4 33.Bxe4 Rxe4 34.Rxe4 Rf1+ 35.Re1 Qf5+ 36.Ka1 Rxh1 37.Rxh1 Qxh3 38.Bd4 Qg2 39.Rg1 Qd2 40.Bxa7 Ne5 41.Bc5 Nd3 42.Ba3 Nb4 43.Bxb4 Qd4+ 44.Kb1 Qxg1+ 0-1

White fianchettos his King Bishop

Illustrative Game 14

GM Mikhail Botvinnik

GM Yelfim Geller

Budapest 1952

1.d4 Nf6 2.c4 g6 3.g3 Bg7 4.Bg2 O-O 5.Nc3 d6 6.Nf3 Nbd7 7.O-O e5 8.e4 exd4 9.Nxd4 Nc5 10.h3 Re8 11.Re1 a5

Black often plays this move in this type of position to prevent b2-b4, hence securing the position of the Knight on c5.

12.Qc2 a4 13.Be3 c6 14.Rad1 Qa5 15.a3?

Weakening the queenside. Better is 15.f4.

15...Nfd7 16.Bf1 Re7 17.f4 Nf6 18.Bf2 Bd7

Threatening 18...Rae8.

19.e5 dxe5 20.fxe5 Ne8 21.Nf3 Bf5 22.Qe2 h5 23.Bd4 Nc7 24.Qf2 N7e6 25.Be3 Rae8 26.Nh4

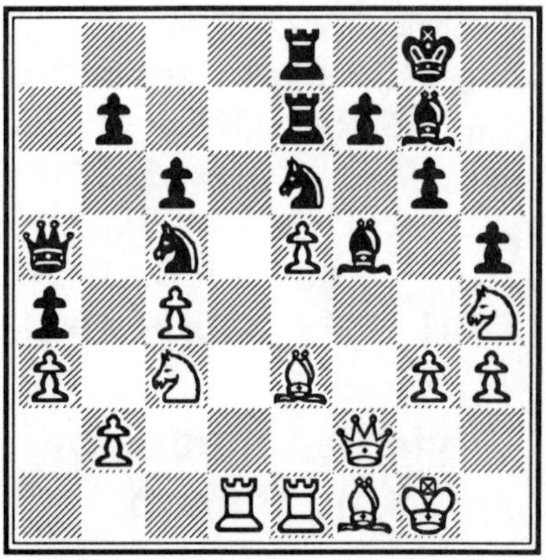

Question 14: Can Black play 26...Ne4?

26...Bxe5 27.Nxf5 gxf5 28.Qxf5 Ng7 29.Qf2 Bxc3 30.bxc3 Ne4 31.Qf4 Nxc3 32.Rc1 Na2 33.Rcd1 Nc3 34.Rc1 Ne4 35.Re2 Qf5 36.g4 hxg4 37.hxg4 Qg6! 38.Rg2 Ng5 39.Qxg5

The only move.

39...Rxe3 40.Qxg6 fxg6 41.c5 Ne6

Not 41...Rxa3 due to 42.Bc4+ Kf8 43.Rf2+ followed by 44.Rf7+.

42.Rb2 Re7 43.Bc4 Kg7 44.Bxe6 R7xe6 45.g5 Rb3 46.Rxb3 axb3 47.Rd1 Re2 0-1

Black's b-pawn cannot be stopped.

Illustrative Game 15

IM Frantisek Zita
GM David Bronstein

Moscow-Prague 1946

1.c4 e5 2.Nc3 Nf6 3.Nf3 d6 4.d4 Nbd7 5.g3 g6 6.Bg2 Bg7 7.O-O O-O 8.b3 c6 9.Bb2 Re8 10.e4 exd4 11.Nxd4 Qb6 12.Qd2?!

Giving up control of the b3-square. Better is 12.Qc2, as 12...Qxd4? is met by 13.Na4.

12...Nc5 13.Rfe1 a5 14.Rab1 a4 15.Ba1 axb3 16.axb3 Ng4!

Taking advantage of the weaknesses at d4, b3 and f2.

17.h3 Rxa1! 18.Rxa1 Nxf2!

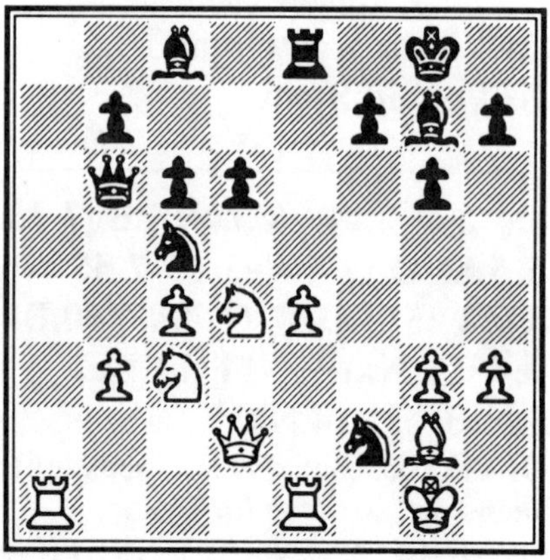

Question 15: If White captures the Knight, how does Black reply?

19.Re3 Nxh3+ 20.Kh2 Nf2!

Threatening 21...Ng4+.

21.Rf3 Ncxe4 22.Qf4 Ng4+ 23.Kh1 f5 24.Nxe4 Rxe4 25.Qxd6 Rxd4 26.Qb8 Rd8 27.Ra8 Be5 28.Qa7 Qb4 29.Qg1 Qf8 30.Bh3 Qh6 0-1

If 31.Qf1, then the quickest way to win is 31...Rd2 32.Rxc8+ Kg7 and there is no defense against 33...Rxh2+ followed by 34...Bd4+.

The King's Indian Defense can also be played against other moves besides 1.d4, as illustrated in the following game by Fischer:

Illustrative Game 16

NM Emil Nikolic
GM Bobby Fischer

Vinkovci 1968

1.c4 g6 2.Nc3 Bg7 3.g3 e5 4.Bg2 d6 5.e3 Nf6 6.Nge2 O-O 7.O-O

It is not good to commit the King so early if White intends to play d4.

7...c6 8.d4

Worth considering is 8.d3.

8...Re8 9.Rb1

9.b4 can be played immediately. 9.dxe5 may be best to avoid the coming kingside attack.

9...e4

Advancing the pawn to e4 and strongpointing it. Fischer and others have won many games with this pattern. With the center blocked, White cannot coordinate his pieces so that he reaches the kingside quickly enough to defend against a sudden sacrificial attack.

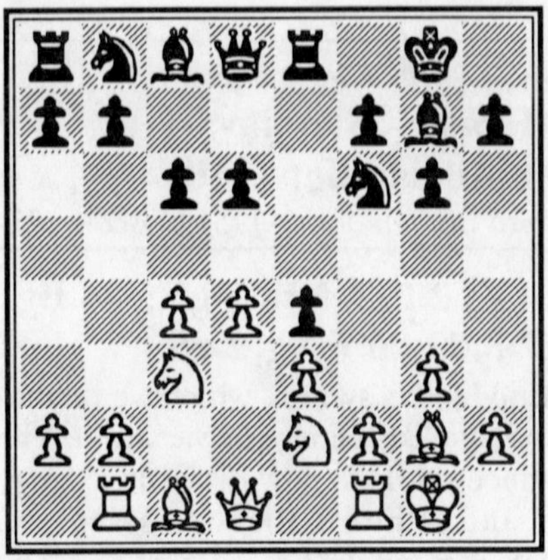

10.b4 Bf5 11.h3 h5 12.Nf4 Nbd7 13.a4 Nf8 14.c5

This blocks the position, making Black's attack even stronger. White's position was already difficult.

14...d5 15.b5 N8h7 16.Bd2 Ng5 17.Rb2 Qd7 18.Kh2 Bh6

A very important move. The Bishop indirectly attacks the Knight on f4 and creates a square for the King on g7.

19.a5

White appears to be breaking through on the queenside, while it is not clear what Black can do on the kingside. But Fischer has seen further.

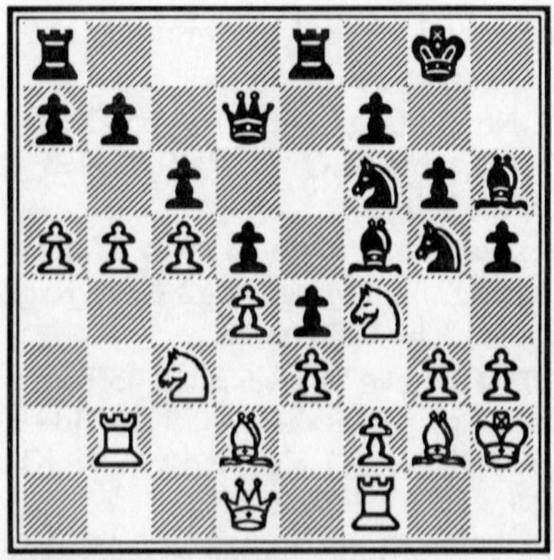

19...Bg4!

Compare this with move 28 of game 2 in the King's Indian Attack chapter. The decisive breakthrough is made by placing the white-squared Bishop en prise. The point here is to strongpoint the f3-square.

20.hxg4

White will not survive long after 20.Qb3 Nf3+ 21.Bxf3 (21.Kh1 Bxf4) 21...Bxf3 22.bxc6 bxc6 23.Qb7 Qf5 24.Qxc6 Bxf4 followed by ...Ng4+.

20...hxg4 21.Rh1 Nf3+ 22.Bxf3 gxf3 23.Kg1 Bxf4 24.exf4 Kg7

White has no defense.

25.f5 Rh8 26.Bh6+ Rxh6 37.Rxh6 Kxh6 28.Qd2+ g5 29.bxc6 Qxf5 30.Nd1 Qh3 31.Ne3 Kg6 0-1

Solutions:

1. 28...Rf7

2. 34...Qg1+ 35.Bxg1 Rxg1+ 36.Kh2 Nxf3#.

3. 27...Bh3+ 28.Rxh3 Rxf2+ 29.Kg3 Qg5#.

4. 26...Bxf1? is a mistake not due to 27.Kxf1? fxe2++ 28.Kg1 Rf1+ 29.Rxf1 Qh1+ 30.Kxh1 exf1=Q#, rather 27.Nf2!

5. 27...Qxg5+ 28.Kf2 Bh6 29.Bc1 Qh4+ wins for Black.

6. 34...Qh1+ 35.Kf2 Qxg2+ 36.Ke3

Nxd5+ and 37...Rxf3+, winning.

7. 33...Qg5 34.Be1 Qg3+.

8. No, 43.Qxg2 Ng3+ 44.Rxg3 hxg3 45.axb6 axb6 46.Qxg3 Ra8 47.Ne3 is good for White.

9. Black has mate in five: 37...f3+ 38.Kh1 g2+ 39.Bxg2 fxg2+ 40.Kxg2 Rf2+ 41.Kh1 Rxh2 mate.

10. 41...Rg4 42.Rg8+ Kh7! 43.Rh8+ Bxh8 44.c8=Q Rxh4+ 45.Kg1 Bd4+ 46.Kf1 Rf2+ 47.Kg1 Rd2+ 48.Kf1 Rh1#.

11. If 31...Rxd5 32.Bxd5 Qxd5, then 33.Qxe8+.

12. 31.Bxg6 hxg6 32.Qh8+ Kf7 33.Rh7+!

13. If 23.Qxe5, then 23...Re7 24.Qc3 Rxe1+ 25.Bxe1 Bb4 26.Qxb4 Rxb4 27.Bxb4 Qe3+ followed by 28...Qf2 winning.

14. If 26...Ne4 27.Nxe4 Bxe4, then 28.Bd2 Qxe5 29.Bc3 wins a piece.

15. If 19.Qxf2, then 19...Nd3 or if 19.Kxf2, then 19...Nxb3.

A Defense to 1.e4: The Sicilian Accelerated Dragon

Second Move Alternatives to 2.Nf3

Illustrative Game 1

GM Vassily Smyslov

GM Mikhail Botvinnik

World Championship (15) Moscow 1954

1.e4 c5 2.Nc3 Nc6 3.g3 g6 4.Bg2 Bg7 5.d3 d6 6.Nge2 e5

Botvinnik's system, which we recommend against the closed variation. The advance d3-d4 is now difficult to carry out and White's Bishop is shut in. Black can meet f2-f4 with f7-f5. The weakness at d5 is of little consequence as Black can control this square with his minor pieces.

7.Nd5

Black also has no problems after 7.O-O Nge7 8.f4 O-O.

7...Nge7

Black has no fear of 8.Bg5 h6 9.Bf6 O-O.

8.c3?

This is the cause of all of White's future problems. Black is now able to get rid of his weakness at d5 and White's advance d3-d4 is also made less effective as it does not open the d-file. Better is 8.N2c3 or 8.Nxe7.

8...Nxd5 9.exd5 Ne7 10.O-O

10.d4 exd4 11.cxd4 cxd4 12.Nxd4 O-O allows Black's King Bishop to become active.

10...O-O 11.f4?!

This only worsens White's position.

The pawn on f4 limits the c1-Bishop and e2-Knight. His King position is also weakened. Better is 11.d4.

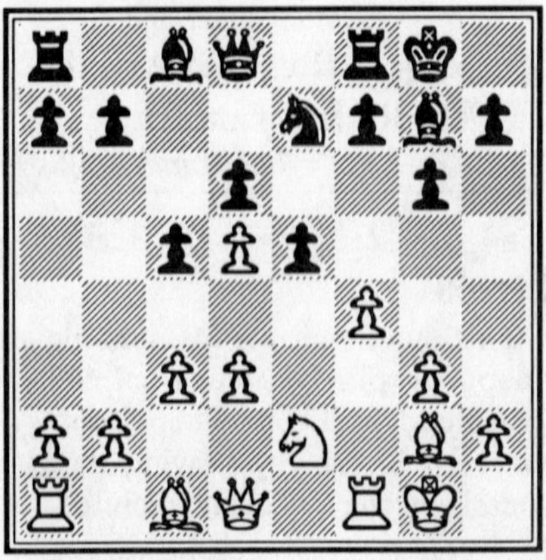

11...Bd7 12.h3

Played against 12...Qc8. 12.fxe5 dxe5 13.d6 Qxd6 14.Bxb7 Rb8 is good for Black.

12...Qc7 13.Be3 Rae8 14.Qd2?!

As will soon become clear, this is a very poor spot for the Queen. Better is 14.Bf2.

14...Nf5 15.Bf2 h5 16.Rae1?!

16.g4 hxg4 17.hxg4 Nh6 18.g5 was White's last chance for freedom. Black prevents this with his next move.

16...Qd8!

Now 17.g4 would be met with 17...hxg4 18.hxg4 Nh4.

17.Kh2

17.fxe5 Bh6 18.Qc2 Ne3 is bad.

17...Bh6

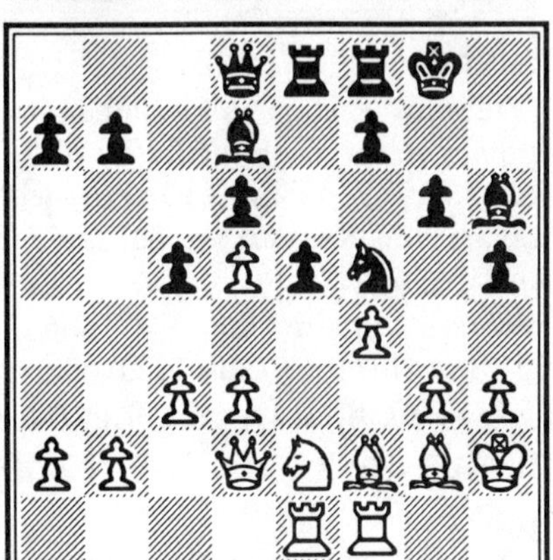

18.h4

Blocking the ...h5-h4 break and thereby hoping to protect the f4-pawn. However, Black is still able to attack this point by means of a combination.

Alternatives are also bad:

a) If 18.g4, then 18...hxg4 19.hxg4 Nh4 20.g5 Nxg2 21.Kxg2 exf4 22.gxh6 Qg5+ 23.Kh2 Qxh6+ 24.Kg1 Qg5+ 25.Kh2 Kg7 followed by 26...Rh8+ is winning.

b) 18.Qc2 exf4 19.Nxf4 h4!

c) 18.Bg1 h4 19.g4 Ng3.

18...Qf6!

There is no defense to 19...exf4 20.Nxf4 Nxh4.

19.Be4

If 19.Bg1, then 19...Nxh4!

19...exf4 20.Nxf4 Nxh4 21.Be3 Nf5

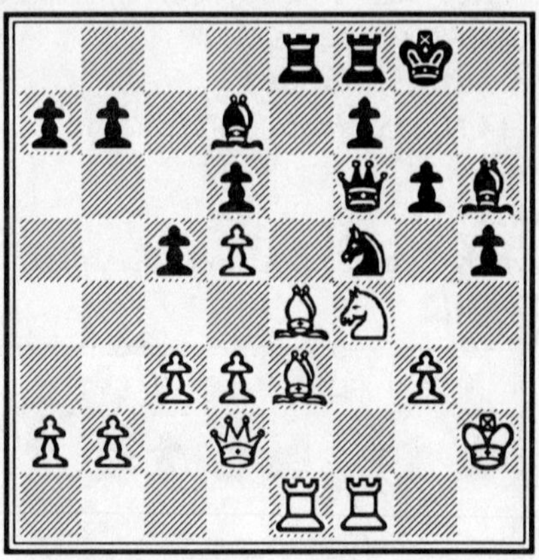

Question 1: Before making his 18th move, Black had calculated a reply to 22.Nxh5. What is it?

22.Bxf5 Qxf5 23.Qg2

23.Ne6 Bxe3! 24.Qxe3 Qxd5 is also hopeless for White.

23...Qg4 24.Qe2 Qxe2+ 25.Rxe2 Re5 26.Ree1 Rfe8 27. Bf2 h4

Creating two connected passed pawns.

28.Rxe5 Rxe5 29.d4 hxg3+ 30. Kxg3 Rg5+ 31.Kh2 Rf5 32.Be3

cxd4 33. cxd4 Kh7

Threatening to win a piece with 34...g5.

34.Rf2 g5 35.Ne2 Rxf2+ 36. Bxf2 f5 0-1

Illustrative Game 2

GM Vladimir Hresc

GM Dusan Rajkovic

Yugoslavia 1988

1.e4 c5 2.c3 Nf6 3.e5 Nd5 4.d4 cxd4 5.Nf3 e6 6.cxd4 d6 7.a3 Bd7 8.Bd3 Bc6 9.O-O Nd7 10.Bg5?!

This weakens the f4-square.

10...Be7 11.Bxe7 Qxe7 12.Nbd2 O-O 13.Nc4?!

Better is 13.g3 Rfd8 14.Qe2 dxe5 15.dxe5 Nc5 16.Bb5 with chances for equality.

13...dxe5 14.dxe5?

14.Nfxe5 Nxe5 15.Nxe5 had to be tried.

14...Nf4

Now White's position falls apart.

15.Qd2

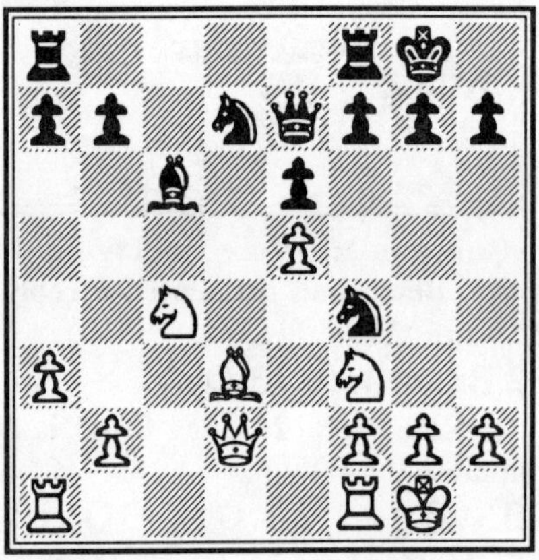

15...Nxg2! 16.Kxg2 Qh4 17.h3 b5 18.Qe3 bxc4 19.Be2 f6 20.exf6 Qxf6 21.Kg3 Bd5 22.Rad1 Rab8 0-1

Alternatives to 3.d4

Illustrative Game 3

GM Miguel Illescas Cordaba

GM Vladimir Kramnik

Alcobendas (m/5) 1993

1.e4 c5 2.Nf3 Nc6 3.Bb5 g6 4.Bxc6

This move became fashionable after Kasparov played it against Salov at Dortmund in 1992. Even Bobby Fischer fell in line by playing it against Spassky in the 1992 return match.

4...bxc6

4...dxc6 releases the pressure in the center. White can either build up for an attack with h3, Nc3, d3, and Be3 followed by queenside castling, or can castle kingside and aim for a small plus.

5.O-O Bg7 6.Re1

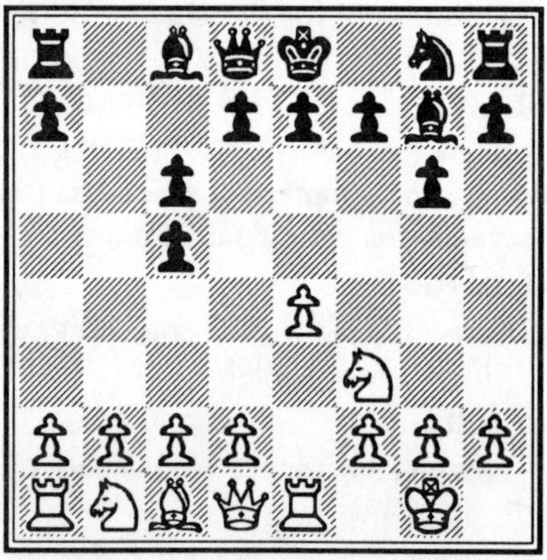

6...Nh6

Dubious is 6...e5 as Fischer scored a brilliant victory with the flashy 7.b4. As well, 7.c3 Ne7 8.d4 was hard to meet in Makarichev–Krasenkov, Tal memorial Moscow 1992.

Worth considering is 6...Nf6 7.e5 Nd5 8.c4 Nc7 9.d4 cxd4 10.Qxd4.

7.c3 O-O 8. d4 cxd4 9.cxd4 d6 10.Nc3 f6 11.b3 Nf7 12.Bb2 Qa5?!

Better is 12...Bd7 followed by ...Rc8

and ...c5, although White would still have a slight advantage.

13.Qc2 Bd7

Not 13...c5? 14.Nd5.

14.Nd2 Rac8 15.Nc4 Qa6 16.Rad1 Be6

Not 16...c5? 17.Nd5 Rfe8 18.e5! with a large advantage to White.

17.Ne3

With the idea of f2-f4.

17...Bh6 18.Qb1 Rfe8 19.d5 cxd5 20.Ncxd5 Kf8?

Correct is 20...Nd8.

21.f4

With the idea of f4-f5.

21...Nd8 22.f5 Bf7 23.Nc4 Bg7 24.Qa1! Kg8

If 24...Nc6, then White has a large advantage after 25.Nxf6 exf6 26.Nxd6.

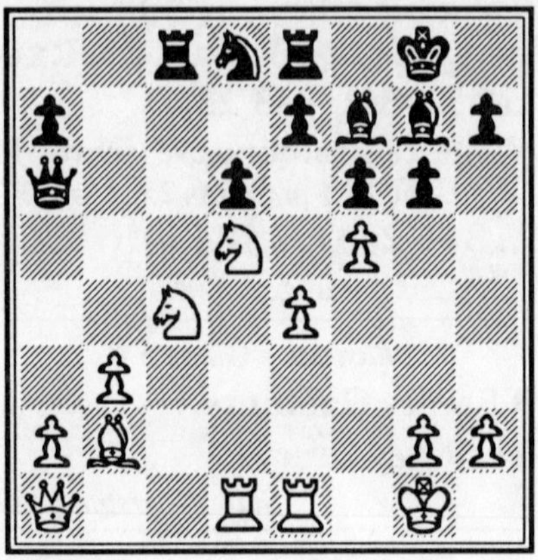

25.Nxf6+!

Not 25.Bxf6? exf6 26.Nxf6+ Bxf6 27.Qxf6 Bxc4 with a large advantage to Black.

25...Bxf6

If 25...exf6, then 26.Nxd6 Nb7 27.Nxc8 Rxc8 28.e5 with a large advantage to White.

26.Bxf6 Bxc4 27.Bh8! e5

The only move.

28.fxe6 Nxe6 29.bxc4 Rf8?

Correct is 29...Rxc4 with a large advantage to White. After the text Black's position is lost.

30.e5 dxe5

If 30...Kxh8, then 31.exd6+ Ng7 32.Re7 Qb6+ 33.Kh1 Rg8 34.d7 Rcf8 35.Rde1 Qd8 36.c5 wins.

31.Rxe5 Rf7 32.Rde1 Nf8 33.c5 Qc4 34.Rc1 Qb4 35.h3 Qd2 36.Ree1?

Short on time, White misses 36.Kh1. After the text he only has a slightly better position.

36...Rxc5 37.Rxc5 Qf2+ 38.Kh1 Qxc5 39.Bd4 Qc2?!

Giving White a large advantage. Correct is 39...Qd5.

40.a3 h5 41.Bg1 Qf5 42.Qa2 Kg7

If 42...Kh7, then 43.Re2.

43.Qb2+ Kh7 44.Re5 Qd3 45.Re8?!

Better is 45.Qb4 with a large advantage. Now Black obtains counterchances.

45...g5! 46.Qe5 Qf5 47.Qxf5+ Rxf5 48.Re7+ Kg6 49.Rxa7 Ne6 50.Ra6?!

Correct is 50.a4 immediately. After 50...Rf1 51.a5 Nf4 52.Kh2 Ra1 53.a6 Ra2 54.Ra8 Rxg2+ 55.Kh1 Ra2 56.a7 Ne2 57.Bf2 White wins.

50...Re5 51.a4 Kf5 52.Rb6?

Once again in time pressure, White misses 52.Ra8 with a large advantage.

52...Re1 53.Rb5+ Kg6 54. Rb6 Kf5 55.Rb5+ Kg6 56.a5 Nf4?

Correct is 56...Ra1. The position is equal after 57.Rb6 Kf5 58.a6 Nc7! 59.a7 Rxa7 60.g4+ hxg4 61.hxg4+ Ke5 62.Rc6 Ra4.

57. Rb6+?

Question 2: Still in time pressure, White does not find the correct move. What is it?

57...Kf5 58.Rb5+ Kg6 59.Rb6+ Kf5 60. Rb5+ Draw

Illustrative Game 4

GM Vlastimil Jansa
GM Ilia Smirin

Peer Gynt 1990

1.e4 c5 2.Nf3 Nc6 3.Bb5 g6 4.O-O Bg7 5.c3 Nf6 6.Re1 O-O 7.h3 e5 8.Na3 d6 9.d4

9.Bxc6 bxc6 10.d3 a5 11.Be3 a4 12.Qc2 Re8 13.Rad1 Be6 14.Qb1 Qb8! 15.d4!? exd4 16.cxd4 d5! gives Black a large advantage, Huebner–Adorjan, Bad Lauterberg 1980.

9...cxd4 10.Bxc6 bxc6 11.cxd4 exd4 12.Nxd4 Bb7

Black's two Bishops give him compensation for the weak center pawns.

13.Nb3 a5 14.Bg5 h6 15.Bh4 g5

Weakening the kingside, especially the f5-square. But Black hopes to create dynamic piece play.

16.Bg3 Re8 17.e5 Nd5 18.Nc4

Of course not 18.exd6 Bxb2.

18...dxe5 19.Bxe5 Bf8

Black must keep control of the important c5-square.

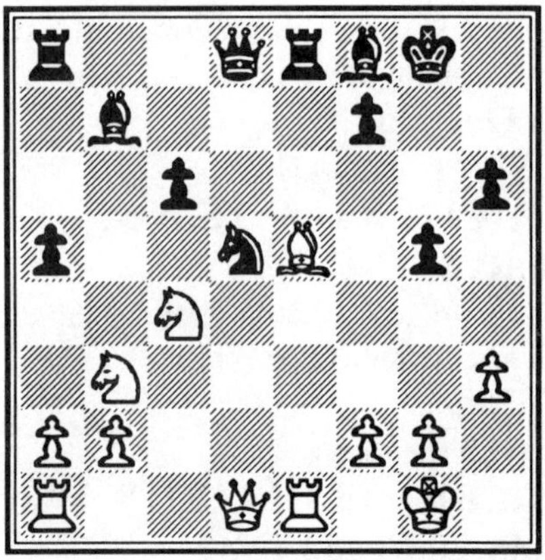

20.Bd4?

It was better to keep control of the f4-square, to stop Black's next move. Better is 20.Nd4, heading to f5.

20...Nf4

Threatening 21...c5.

21.Ncxa5?!

Too greedy. Better is 21.Bb6.

21...Qd5 22.f3 Ba6 23.Rxe8 Rxe8 24.Bf2 Nd3 25.a3

White can hardly move any of his pieces. The text prevents 25...Bb4.

25...Bd6 26.Qd2 Bf4 0-1

...Nxf2 is coming.

Illustrative Game 5

IM Sergey Galdunts
GM Alexey Dreev

Saint Petersburg 1993

1.e4 c5 2.Nf3 Nc6 3.Bb5 g6 4.O-O Bg7 5.c3 Nf6 6.Re1 O-O 7.h3 e5 8. Bxc6?!

Better is 8.d3.

8...dxc6 9.Nxe5

9.d4?! cxd4 10.cxd4 exd4 11.e5 Nd7 is slightly better for Black.

9...Re8 10.f4 Nh5

Previously played was 10...Nxe4 11.Rxe4 f6 12.Qb3+ Be6 13.Nc4 Bd5! with a large advantage to Black, Weingold–Kapengut, Minsk 1975.

11.d4 Qh4 12.Rf1

Not 12.Nf3? Qg3 followed by ...Bxh3.

12...Bxh3! 13.gxh3 Qg3+ 14.Kh1 Qxh3+ 15.Kg1 Ng3

Playing for the win instead of repeating moves with 15...Qg3+.

16.Nd2 Qh1+ 17.Kf2

17...Qh2+?!

Better is 17...Nxf1! Black would then have a big advantage.

18.Kf3 Qh3 19.Kf2

Question 3: What should Black play against 19.Rg1?

19...Nxf1 20.Nxf1 cxd4 21.cxd4 f6 22.Nf3 Rxe4 23.Ng3 Re7 24.f5 g5 25.Qb3+ Kh8 26.Bd2 Rae8 27.Qd3

Correct is 27.Rh1 Re2+ 28.Nxe2 Qxh1 29.Ng3 Qh3 30.Qf7 Rf8 31.Qh5! Qxh5 32.Nxh5 Re8 with an equal position.

27...g4 28.Rh1 Re2+ 29.Nxe2 Qxh1 30.Ne1 h5 31.Nf4 h4 32.Ne6 g3+ 33. Ke2 g2 34.Be3 Bh6 35.Kd1 Bxe3 36. Qxe3 g1=Q 0-1

The Acclerated Dragon

Illustrative Game 6

NM Danny Kopec

NM Larry Christiansen

USA 1972.

1.e4 c5 2.Nf3 Nc6 3.d4 cxd4 4.Nxd4 g6 5.Nc3 Bg7 6.Be3 Nf6 7.Bc4 Qa5

Preventing White from castling queenside, as 8.Qd2? would be met by 8...Nxe4.

8.f3?! Qb4 9.Bb3?

It's equal after 9.Nxc6 bxc6.

9...Nxe4 10.Nxc6

If 10.fxe4, then 10...Bxd4 11.Bxd4 Qxd4 12.Qf3 e6 winning, Matulovic–Toran, Palma de Mallorca 1967.

10...Bxc3+ 11.bxc3 Qxc3+ 12.Ke2 dxc6! 13.Bd4

If 13.fxe4, then 13...Bg4+. Or if 13.Qg1, then 13...Nf6 14.Bd4 Qb4 15.Qe3 O-O 16.Rad1 b6! wins.

13...e5!

After this beautiful move White must go into an endgame two pawns down.

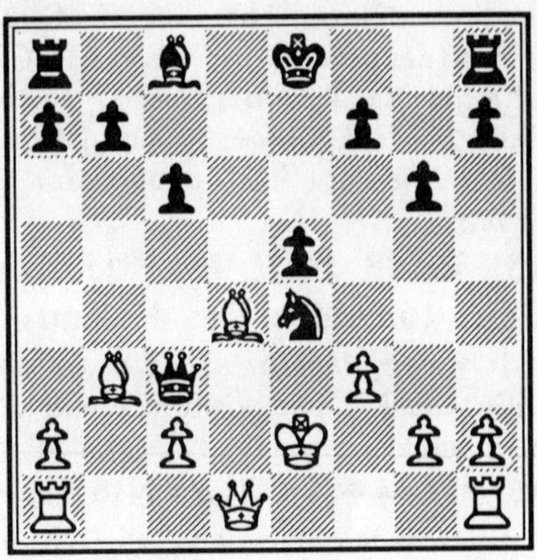

14.Bxc3 Nxc3+ 15.Kf2 Nxd1+ 16.Raxd1 Ke7 17.Rhe1 f6 18.f4 Bg4 19.Rd3 Rad8 20.Rde3 Rd2+ 21.Kg3 Be6 22.fxe5 f5 23.Bxe6 Kxe6 24.Rb3 b6 25.Ra3 Rhd8 26.Rxa7 Rxc2 27.Rb7 Rd3+ 28.Kh4 Rxg2 29.h3 Rd4+ 0-1

Illustrative Game 7

Ekblom

IM Krzysztof Pytel

Correspondence 1969

1.e4 c5 2.Nf3 Nc6 3.d4 cxd4 4.Nxd4 g6 5.Nc3 Bg7 6.Be3 Nf6 7.Bc4 Qa5 8. O-O O-O 9.Bb3 d6 10.h3 Bd7 11.f4 Nxd4 12.Bxd4 Bc6 13.Qd3

The strongest move. Alternatives are:

1) 13.Qe1 (This move forces a draw, one of the drawbacks of this variation.) 13...Qb4 (Black must counterattack vigorously, otherwise he will be at a disadvantage.) 14.Rd1 Nxe4 15.Bxg7 Kxg7 16.Nd5 Qc5+ 17.Kh2 Nf6 18.Nc7 Bxg2 19.Qxe7 Bxh3 20.Kxh3 Qh5+ Draw by perpetual check.

2) 13.Qe2?! (This looks similar to the last variation. However, the Queen is better placed on e1.) 13...Qb4 14.Rfd1 Nxe4 15.Bxg7 Kxg7 16.Nd5 Bxd5 17.Rxd5 Qb6+ 18.Kh2 Nf6 and White does not have enough for the pawn.

13...Rad8 14.f5 Nd7 15.Bxg7 Kxg7 16.Qd4+ Qe5 17.Rad1?!

It was better to take the sacrifice with 17.Qxa7. The position would have been unclear after 17...Nc5 18.Rae1 e6.

17...Qxd4+ 18.Rxd4 Nf6

Black is better because the advance f4-f5 is bad in the endgame. For example, the e5-square is weak. However, White's next move weakens his pawn structure even more.

19.g4? g5

Fixing White's pawns on the same colored-square as his Bishop.

20.Rfd1 Nd7 21.Nd5 Bxd5 22.Rxd5

Now we have a bad Bishop versus strong Knight.

22...Rc8 23.c3 Kf6 24.Kf2 Ne5 25.Kg3 h5 26.R1d2 Rh8?

Better is first 26...hxg4 27.hxg4 Rh8. White is now able to put up resistance with his next move.

27.Bd1

In order to meet ...hxg4 with Bxg4.

27...Nc4 28.Rf2 Ne3 29.Rd3 hxg4 30.Bxg4 Nxg4 31.hxg4 Rh4 32.Rd5 Rch8

Black is still much better due to his active Rooks and his King will eventually be able to penetrate via the e5-square.

33.Rg2 Rh1 34.Rdd2

This gives the e5-square to Black. But otherwise 34...R8h3+ 35.Kf2 Rb1 was coming.

34...Ke5 35.a4 R8h3+ 36.Kf2 Kf4

36...Kxe4 37.Re2+ would give White too many counterchances.

37.f6

White must try to complicate the position.

37...Rf3+ 38.Ke2 Re3+ 39.Kf2 Ree1

Threatening 40...Rhf1#.

40.Rh2 Rhf1+ 41.Kg2 exf6 42.Rh7 Ke3 0-1

Illustrative 8

NM Turham Yilmaz

GM Borislav Ivkov

Praia de Rocha 1978

1.e4 c5 2.Nf3 Nc6 3.d4 cxd4 4.Nxd4 g6 5.Nc3 Bg7 6.Be3 Nf6 7.Bc4 Qa5 8.O-O O-O 9.Bb3 d6 10.h3 Bd7 11.f4 Nxd4 12.Bxd4 Bc6 13.Qd3 Rad8 14.Nd5 e5

Safer is 14...Nxd5 15.exd5 Bxd4+ 16.Qxd4 Bd7 17.Rae1 Rfe8 18.Kh1 Qc5 19.Qd2 a5 with equality, Klovan–Kapengut, Latvian Championship 1965. Also worth considering according to Silman is 14...Rfe8.

15.Nxf6+ Bxf6 16.Bc3 Qc5+ 17.Kh1 Bg7 18.f5 Bh6

Worth considering are 18...d5 or 18...Bb5.

19.fxg6 hxg6 20.Qg3

Threatening 21.Qxg6+.

20...Kg7 21.Bxf7?

This is unsound. Better is 21.Rad1. Then 21...Bxe4? could be met with 22.Rxf7+ Rxf7 23.Bxf7 Kxf7 24.Qh4.

21...Rxf7 22.Rxf7+ Kxf7 23. Qh4 Rh8 24.Rf1+

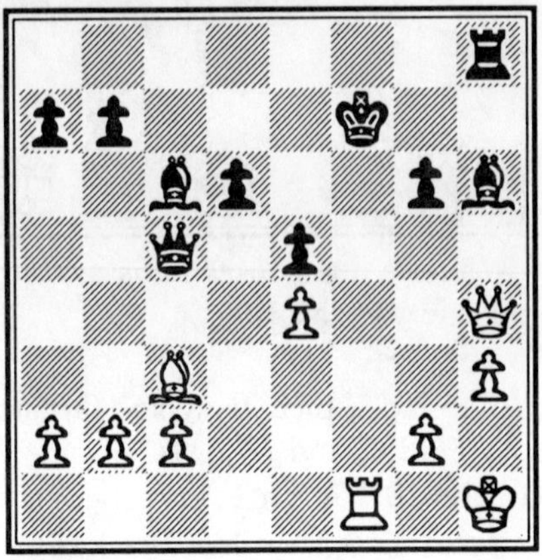

Black must avoid 24...Kg7? 25.Qe7+.

Question 4: What would happen if he plays 24...Kg8?

24...Ke8 25.Qg4 Rf8

25.Qf6 Rf8 would lead to the same variation as the actual game.

26.Qxg6+ Ke7 27.Rxf8 Bxf8 28.Qg5+?

It was better to get the Bishop into the game with 28.Be1. However, after 28...d5 29.Bh4+ Kd7 30.Qf5+ Kc7 31.Qxe5+ Kb6 Black has a clear advantage.

28...Ke8 29.Qg6+ Kd8 30.Qg8 Qf2 31.Qc4 Bh6 32.Ba5+ Kd7 0-1

Illustrative Game 9

NM Martin Gonzalez

IM Juan Manuel Bellon Lopez

Olot 1974

1.e4 c5 2.Nf3 g6 3.d4 cxd4 4.Nxd4 Bg7 5.Nc3 Nc6 6.Be3 Nf6 7.Bc4 Qa5 8. O-O O-O 9.Bb3 d6 10.h3 Bd7 11.f4 Nxd4 12.Bxd4 Bc6 13.Qd3 Rad8 14.Rad1 Nd7 15.Bxg7 Kxg7 16.Kh1 Nc5 17.Qd4+ e5 18.fxe5 Nxb3 19.axb3 dxe5 20.Qf2 f5

Not 20...Rxd1 21.Qf6+ Kg8 22.Rxd1.

21.b4

Deflecting Black's Queen away from the d8-square. If 21.Rxd8, then 21...Qxd8 22.Qxa7 fxe4 23.Rxf8 Qxf8 24.Qe3 (24.Nd1? e3 25.Nxe3 Qf2 wins for Black) 24...Qf4 25.Nd1 Qf1+ 26.Qg1 Qe2 27.Ne3 h5 with advantage to Black.

21...Qxb4 22.Rxd8 Rxd8 23.exf5 g5

An improvement over 23...Qf4 24.Qe1 with a large advantage to White, Shagalovich–Baumbach, Byelorussia–East Germany 1968. Black is better because his Bishop controls a powerful diagonal.

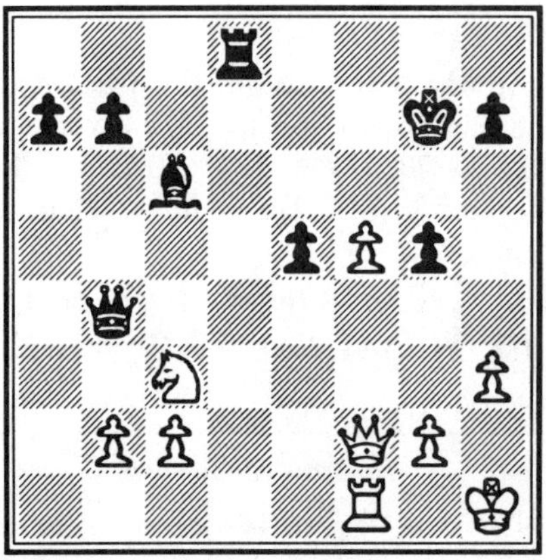

24.f6+ Kf7 25.Qe3 Qh4 26.Kh2

Question 5: How does Black reply to 26.Qxe5?

26...g4 27.Qxe5 g3+ 28.Qxg3

Black wins in the endgame after 28.Kg1 Qd4+.

28...Qxg3+ 29.Kxg3 Rg8+ 30.Kf4 Rxg2

Black wins because his Bishop and Rook are much better than White's Knight and Bishop and White's pawns are weak.

31.Ke5 Rg3 32.h4 Re3+ 33.Kf4 Rh3 34.Rf2 Rxh4+ 35.Kg5 Rh1 36.Ne2 h6+ 37.Kf5 Rh5+ 38.Kg4 Rg5+ 39.Kh4 Rg2 40.Rxg2 Bxg2 41.Nf4 Bf3 42.Kg3 Bd1 43.c3 Kxf6 44.Nd5+ Ke5 45.Ne3 Bh5 46.Kh4 Be2 47.Kg3 Ke4 48.Kf2 Bb5 49.c4 Bd7 50.Ke2 a5 51. Kd2 Kd4 52.b3 h5 53.Ng2 Bf5 54.Nf4 h4 55.Ng2 h3 56.Ne3 Ke4 57.Ke2 Kf4 58.Nf1 Bc2 0-1

Illustrative Game 10

IM Roland Ekstrom

GM Ognjen Cvitan

Bern 1988

1.e4 c5 2.Nc3 Nc6 3.Nge2 g6 4.d4 cxd4 5.Nxd4 Bg7 6.Be3 Nf6 7.Be2 O-O 8.Qd2?

This allows Black to play a powerful thrust in the center.

8...d5 9.exd5

9.Nxc6 bxc6 10.e5 Ng4 11.Bxg4 Bxg4 12.f4 f6 13.exf6 Bxf6 14.Bd4 e5 is also good for Black.

9...Nxd5 10.Nxd5

Possibly a lesser evil is 10.Nxc6, although after 10...bxc6 11.Rd1 Be6 12.Bd4 Bxd4 13.Qxd4 Qa5 14.Qa4 Qb6 15.Qa3 Rfb8 Black has a slight advantage in Barczay–Adorjan, Budapest 1978

10...Qxd5 11.Bf3 Qc4 12.Be2 Qd5 13.Bf3 Qe5 14. Nxc6 bxc6 15.Bxc6 Ba6

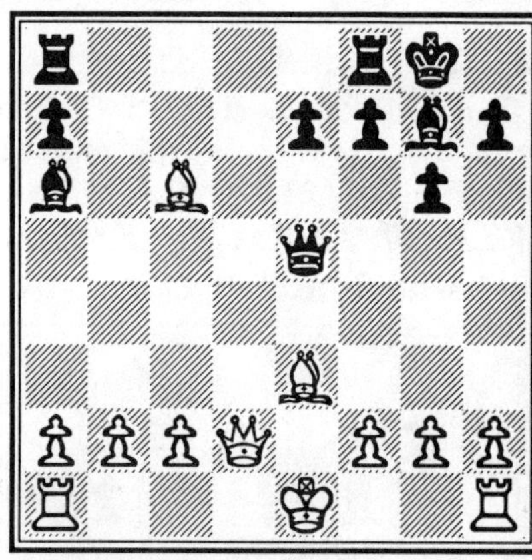

White is doomed as he is unable to find safety for his King.

16.c3

If 16.Bxa8, then 16...Qxb2 threatens both 17...Bc3 and 17...Qxa1+.

16...Rfd8 17. Qc1

Question 6: How does Black reply to 17.Bxa8?

17...Rac8 18.f4

If 18.Bf3, then 18...Rxc3 19.bxc3 Qxc3+ wins. The text creates an escape square for the King at f2.

18...Qa5 19.Bf3 Bxc3+ 20. bxc3 Rxc3 21.Kf2 Rdd3

21...Rxc1 is also possible, but Black

wants more.

22.Qb2 Rxe3 23. Rhe1 Qc5 24.Kg3 e5 25.Qb8+ Kg7 26. fxe5 Be2 27.e6 Rxf3+ 28.gxf3 Rxf3+ 29.Kg2 Rf2+ 30.Kh3 Qh5+ 0-1

Illustrative Game 11

IM Nikolay Minev

GM Paul Keres

Munich Olympiad 1958

1.e4 c5 2.Nf3 g6 3.d4 cxd4 4.Nxd4 Bg7 5.Nc3 Nc6 6.Be3 Nf6 7.Be2 O-O 8. O-O d5 9.exd5 Nb4 10.d6

Worth considering is 10.Nb3 Nfxd5 11.Nxd5 Nxd5 12.Bd4 Nf4 13.Bf3 Bxd4 14.Qxd4 with a slight advantage to White according to Kortchnoi

10...Qxd6 11.Ncb5

Bad is 11.Nbd5 Qb8 12.Bf3 Nc6 with advantage to Black.

11...Qb8 12.Qc1

Perhaps preferable is 12.c4 Nc6 13.Nxc6 bxc6 14.Nd4 and now Black should play 14...Qc7 instead of 14...Qxb2 15.Nxc6 Be6 16.Nxe7+ in Estevez–Andres, Cuban Championship 1984/85.

12...a6 13.Nc3 Nfd5 14.Nxd5 Nxd5 15.Bc4 Nxe3 16.Qxe3 Qc7

Keres' possession of the two Bishops give him the advantage.

17.Bb3 b5 18.Bd5 Rb8 19.c3 e6 20.Bf3 Bd7 21.Rac1 Rfc8 22.Rfd1 a5

Black's minority attack will leave White with a pawn weakness on the queenside.

23.h3 Be8 24.Rc2 Qb6 25.Qc1 Rc7 26.a3 Rbc8 27. Nb3 b4 28.axb4 Ba4 29.Rcd2

Question 7: Can Black play 29...Bxb3?

29...axb4 30.Rd8+ Bf8 31.Qh6 Be8 32.Qf4 bxc3 33. bxc3 Rxc3

Not 33...Qxb3 34.Rxe8 Rxe8 35.Qxc7.

34.Rxc8 Rxc8 35.Nd2 Rd8 36. Rb1 Qd6 37.Qxd6 Bxd6 38.Ne4 Be7 39.g3?

This loses a piece. As all the pawns are on one side of the board, White could have put up some resistance, although the defense would have been difficult.

39...f5 40.Nc3 Rd3 0-1

Illustrative Game 12

NM Alan LaVergue

IM John Donaldson

Reno 1987

1.e4 c5 2.Nf3 Nc6 3.d4 cxd4 4.Nxd4 g6 5.Be3 Nf6 6.Nc3 Bg7

7.Be2 O-O 8. O-O

Better is 8.Nb3 to stop Black's next move.

8...d5 9.exd5 Nxd5 10.Nxd5 Qxd5!? 11.Bf3 Qa5!

This pawn sacrifice offers Black lots of chances.

12.Nxc6 bxc6 13.c3

13.Bxc6 Rb8 is good for Black.

13...Rb8 14.Qc1

Forced.

14...c5 15.Rd1 Be6 16.Qc2

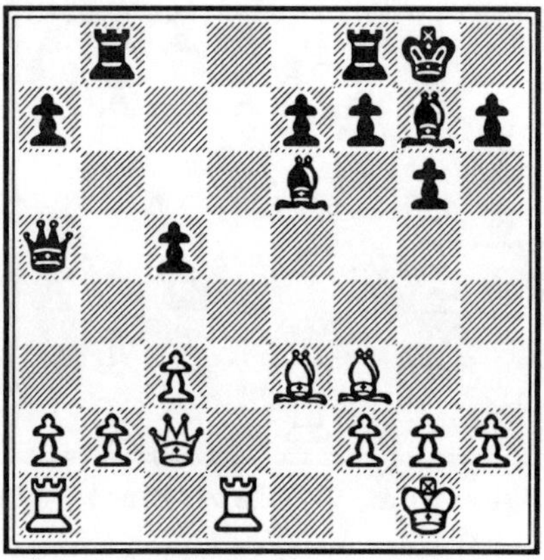

16.Bd5 Bg4 leads to unclear play.

16...c4 17.Bd4?

This attempt to simplify is premature.

17...Bf5 18.Be4 Bxe4 19.Qxe4 Bxd4 20.Qxd4 Rxb2 21.Qxc4 Qb6

Black is better because of White's weakness at c3 to hit and Black's greater piece activity.

22.Qf4?!

Here 22.Qd4, trying to obtain a Rook and 3 pawns versus Rook and 4 pawns was the best drawing chance.

22...Rc8 23.Rac1 Rxa2 24.Re1 e6 25.Rcd1 Qc7 26.Qf6

26...Ra6

Covering the e6-square. Not 26...Ra5 27.Rxe6.

27.h4 h5

To stop h4-h5-h6. Black's a-pawn will prove decisive.

28.Re4 Rd6 29.Red4 Qxc3 30.Qf4 Rxd4 31.Rxd4 Qc1+ 0-1

Illustrative Game 13

NM Rudolf Osterman

GMC Gennady Nesis

Correspondence 1980

1.e4 c5 2.Nf3 d6 3.d4 cxd4 4.Nxd4 Nf6 5.Nc3 g6 6.Be2 Bg7 7.Be3 Nc6 8.Nb3 O-O 9.f4 Be6 10.g4 Na5 11.g5 Nd7 12.Bd4 f6

Opening the f-file. Also, Black wants to keep his King Bishop for defensive purposes.

13.gxf6 Nxf6 14.Rg1

Worth considering is 14.Qd2 Rc8 15.f5 gxf5 16.Rg1 Nc6 17.exf5 Bxf5 18.Qg5 Bg6 19.O-O-O with compensation, Aseev–Ionov, Leningrad 1986.

14...Bf7 15.Qd2 Rc8 16.f5 Qc7 17.h4 Nc4 18.Bxc4 Qxc4

Black's kingside is well fortified and White will find it hard to break through. In the meantime Black will counterattack on the queenside.

19.h5 Nxh5 20.Bxg7 Kxg7 21.Nd4

Threatening 22.fxg6 followed by 23.Nf5+.

21...Kh8 22.O-O-O Rg8 23.Rge1

Threatening 24.e5.

23...Rc5 24.Qh6 Nf6 25.Nf3 gxf5 26.Rd4 Qe6 27.exf5 Qxf5

White does not have enough compensation for the two pawns that he has sacrificed.

28.Rf4 Qg6 29.Qxg6 Bxg6 30.Rxe7 Rxc3

This little combination quickly ends the game.

31.bxc3 Nd5 32.Rff7 Nxe7 33.Rxe7 Rg7 34.Re6 Rd7 35.Nd4 Bf7 0-1

Illustrative Game 14

NM Vsevolod Rauzer

GM Mikhail Botvinnik

USSR 1933

1.e4 c5 2.Nf3 d6 3.d4 cxd4 4.Nxd4 Nf6 5.Nc3 g6 6.Be2 Bg7 7.Be3 Nc6 8.Nb3 O-O 9.f4 Be6 10.O-O Na5 11.Nxa5 Qxa5 12.Bf3

a) 12.Qd2 Rac8 13.Rad1 Rfe8 14.Bf3 Rc4 15.Qe2 Rec8 is at most slightly better for Black.

b) 12.Bd4 Rac8 13.Bf3 Rc4 14.a3 b5 15.Be2 Rxd4 16.Qxd4 Ng4 17.Qd2 Qb6+ is slightly better for Black, Eoljan–Doncenko, Erevan 1977.

12...Bc4 13.Re1

13.Rf2 Rfd8 14.Qd2 Qc7 15.b3 Ba6 16.Rad1 Rac8 17.Nd5 Nxd5 18.exd5 Bc3 with a large advantage to Black, Treybal–Foltys, Czechoslovakia 1940.

13...Rfd8 14.Qd2 Qc7 15.Rac1

More active is 15.Qf2

15...e5 16.b3?

Better is 16.fxe5 dxe5 17.Qf2 b6 18.g4 h6 with equality.

16...d5! 17.exd5 e4 18.bxc4 exf3 19.c5 Qa5 20.Red1

Better is 20.Qd3 although Black is much better after 20...b6.

20...Ng4 21.Bd4 f2+ 22.Kf1 Qa6+ 23.Qe2 Bxd4 24.Rxd4 Qf6 25.R1d1 Qh4 26.Qd3 Re8 27.Re4 f5 28.Re6 Nxh2+ 29.Ke2 Qxf4 0-1

Illustrative Game 15

IM Blas Lugo

IM Miquel Andres

Havana 1988

1.e4 c5 2.Nf3 Nc6 3.d4 cxd4 4.Nxd4 g6 5.Nc3 Bg7 6.Be3 Nf6 7.f3 O-O 8.Bc4 Qb6 9.Bb3 Nxe4 10.Nd5 Qa5+ 11.c3 Nc5 12.Nxc6 dxc6 13.Nxe7+ Kh8 14.Nxc8 Re8 15.Nd6 Rxe3+ 16.Kf2 Re7 17.Re1

Better than 17.Nxf7+ Rxf7 18.Bxf7 Qb6! (also worth considering is 18...Rd8!? 19.Qe2 Nd3+ 20.Kf1 Nxb2! 21.Qxb2? Bxc3 22.Qc1 Rd2+) 19.Kf1 Qxb2 20.Rb1 Qxc3 21.Rc1 Qb4 with compensation for the Exchange.

17...Qb6!

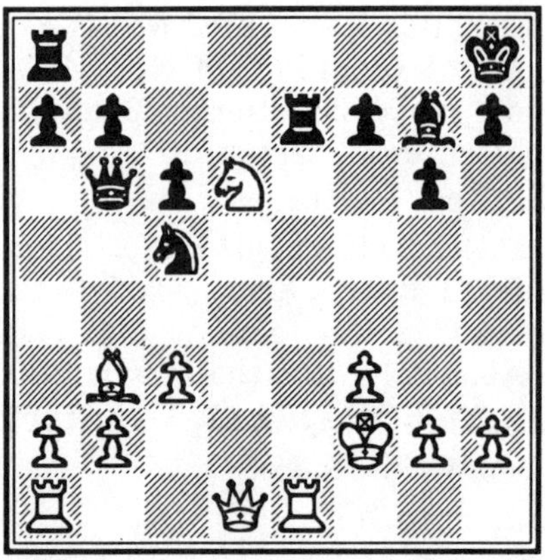

Question 8: What should happen after 18.Rxe7.

18.Kf1 Rxe1+ 19.Qxe1 Nxb3 20.Nxf7+?

Better is 20.axb3. And now rather then 20...Qxb3? 21.Rxa7 Rf8 22.Rxb7 Qd5 23.Ne4! with advantage to White, Black should play 20...Rf8! 21.Qe7 (21.b4 Qc7) 21...Qxb3 22.Qxb7 Qd5 23.Ne4 Bh6! with an unclear position.

20...Kg8 21.Qe6 Qb5+ 22.Kf2 Qd5 23.Nh6+ Kf8 24.Qxd5 cxd5 25.axb3 Bxh6 0-1

Illustrative Game 16

IM Sofia Polgar
IM Peter Leko

Budapest 1993

1.e4 c5 2.Nf3 Nc6 3.d4 cxd4 4.Nxd4 g6 5.c4

The Maroczy bind.

5...Nf6 6.Nc3 d6 7.Be2 Nxd4 8.Qxd4 Bg7 9.Bg5 Qa5

Forcing Qd2, after which Black will be able to exchange Queens when Nd5 is played.

10.Qd2 O-O 11.f3 Be6 12.Rc1 Rfc8 13.b3 a6

14...b5 is threatened, therefore White goes into an endgame.

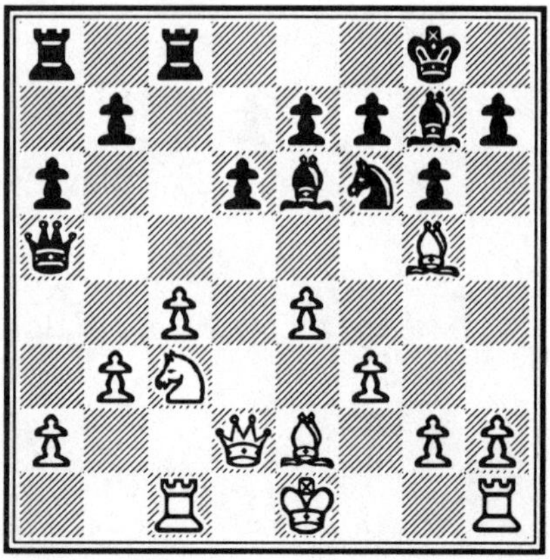

14.Na4 Qxd2+ 15.Kxd2 Nd7

In the game Karpov–Kavalek, Nice Olympiad 1974, Black got a cramped position after 15...Rc6 16.Nc3 Rac8 17.Nd5. 17...Nxd5 is impossible and 17...Bxd5 gives White the Bishop pair.

16.g4

Of course not 16.Bxe7 because of 16...Bh6+.

16...Kf8 17.Be3 Rab8 18.g5 f5

Not 18...b5? 19.cxb5 Rxc1 20.Rxc1 axb5 21.Bxb5.

19.exf5?!

Activating Black's Queen Bishop. Correct is 19.gxf6 Bxf6 20.Nc3.

19...Bxf5 20.f4?!

Better is 20.Nc3 to stop 20...b5.

20...b5! 21.cxb5 axb5 22.Nc3 Nc5! 23.Bxc5

If 23.Nxb5, then 23...Ra8 24.Nc3 Bxc3+ 25.Kxc3 Nd3+.

23...Rxc5 24.b4 Rc6 25.Bd3?

Now White is lost. Better is 25.Nxb5, although Black's position is very good after 25...Ra6 26.a3 Bd7.

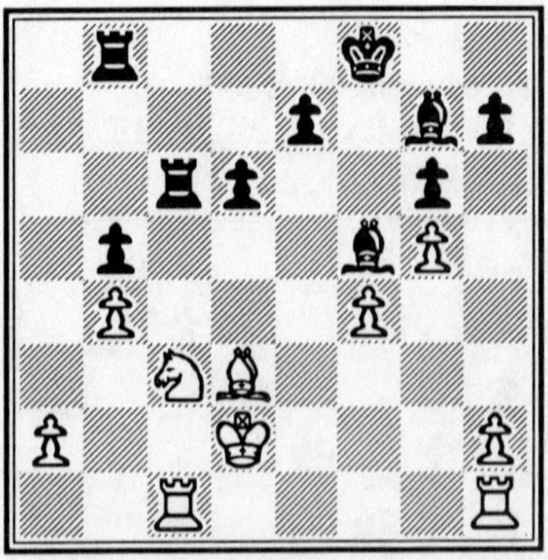

25...Bxd3 26.Kxd3 Rc4 27.a3

27.Rhf1 would have offered more resistance. Now Black gets two connected passed pawns.

27...Rxf4 28.Rhf1 Rxf1 29.Rxf1+ Ke8 30.Rf4 Bxc3 31.Kxc3 Rc8+ 32.Kb3 e5 33.Rh4 Rc7 34.a4 bxa4+ 35.Kxa4 Re7 36.Re4 d5 37.Re1 Kd7 38.Kb3 Kd6 39.Ra1 e4 40.Kc3 Ke5 41.b5 d4+ 42.Kd2 Rf7 0-1

Solutions:

1. 18...gxh5 23.Bxf5 (if 23.Bxh6, then 23...Qxh6) 23...Bxe3 24.Rxe3 Qg5! winning the Exchange.

2. 57.Kh2! For example, 57...Re2 58.a6 Rg2+ 59.Kh1 Ra2 60.a7 Nxh3 61.Be3 g4 62.Rb8 g3 63.Rg8+ Kf5 64.Rxg3 Nf4 65.Rg8 wins.

3. 19...Ne4!

4. 25.Qd8+ Kh7 26.Rf7+ Bg7 27.Qe7 Rg8 28.Qh4#.

5. 26...Qxh3+.

6. 17...Rxd2 18.Kxd2 Qb8.

7. No, because of 30.Rd8+ Bf8 31.Qh8 winning.

8. White is in a mating net after 18...Ne4+ 19.Ke2 Qf2+ 20.Kd3 Nc5+ 21.Kc4 b5+ 22.Nxb5 cxb5+ 23.Kxb5 Nxb3 24.axb3 Qb6+.

Further Tips on How to Improve

The Role of the Pieces

Knowing how to use the pieces is a cornerstone of chess strategy. You must be aware of the specific needs of each piece.

The Knight

The Knight, being a short-range piece, is usually stronger in the center than on the side of the board. It is especially strong at an outpost, where it cannot be attacked by the opponent's pawns. In the following game the Knight finds an extremely strong post at the c4-square.

Illustrative Game 1

GM Jose Capablanca

GM Alexander Alekhine

World Championship Buenos Aires 1927

1.d4 d5 2.c4 e6 3.Nc3 Nf6 4.Bg5 Nbd7 5.e3 Be7 6.Nf3 O-O 7.Rc1

Placing the Rook on a file that will later be opened. White postpones the development of his King Bishop in order to save a tempo, as Black is planning ...dxc4.

7...a6

Preparing to play ...dxc4 followed by

...b5.

8.a3?!

A tame move.

8...h6 9.Bh4 dxc4 10.Bxc4 b5 11.Be2 Bb7 12.O-O c5 13.dxc5 Nxc5 14.Nd4 Rc8 15.b4?

Unnecessarily weakening the c4-square. Better is 15.Bf3.

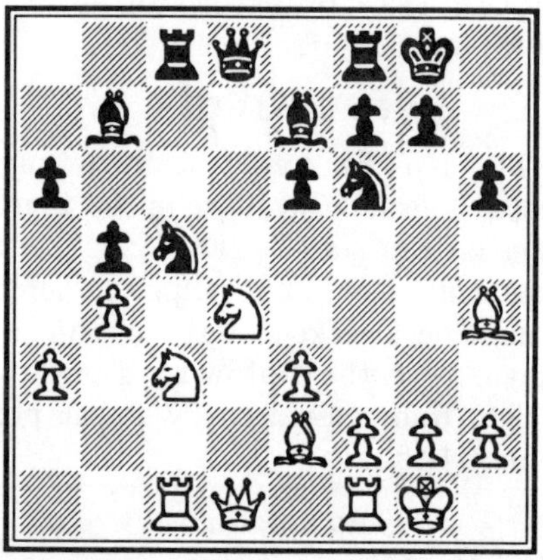

15...Ncd7!

Black is planning ...Nb6-c4.

16.Bg3 Nb6 17.Qb3 Nfd5 18.Bf3 Rc4

Better than 18...Nc4 19.Rfd1 with pressure on the d5-Knight.

19.Ne4 Qc8 20.Rxc4?

Allowing the Knight to occupy c4. Better is 20.Qb1.

20...Nxc4 21.Rc1 Qa8!

Exerting pressure on the a8-h1 diagonal. 22...Nxb4 or 22...Ndxe3 are threatened.

22.Nc3 Rc8

Threatening 23...Nd2.

23.Nxd5 Bxd5 24.Bxd5 Qxd5 25.a4 Bf6

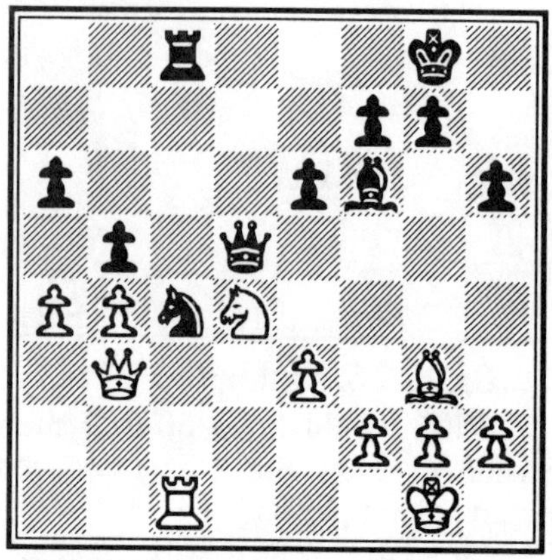

Question 1: How does Black reply to 26.Rd1

26.Nf3 Bb2!

Black wants to play ...e6-e5 without restricting his Bishop.

27.Re1 Rd8 28.axb5 axb5 29.h3

White needs to have an escape square for his King because of possible back-rank mates.

29...e5 30.Rb1 e4 31.Nd4 Bxd4 32.Rd1

32.exd4 would have held out longer, although he will eventually lose after 32...Qxd4.

Question 2: How does Black finish off the game?

The Bishop

The Bishop, being a long-range piece, is strongest on long diagonals and, whenever possible, should not be blocked by its own pawns. They are especially strong when used in pairs. The weakness of the Bishop is that it's doomed to stay on the same colored-square the entire game and can be blocked in by its own pawns, in which case it is called a bad Bishop.

Illustrative Game 2

A Medina
GM Mikhail Botvinnik

Palma de Mallorca 1967

1.e4 d6 2.d4 Nf6 3.Nc3 g6 4.Nf3 Bg7 5.Bc4 c6 6.Bb3 O-O 7.Qe2 Bg4 8.h3 Bxf3 9.Qxf3 e6 10.Bg5 h6 11.Bh4 Nbd7 12.O-O-O

The King will be exposed to attack on the queenside. Better is 12.O-O.

12...Qa5 13.Qe2 b5 14.f4

Weakening the e4-square, which Black immediately exploits.

14...b4 15.Nb1 d5 16.Nd2 c5 17.Bxf6

After this exchange, Black's Bishop becomes a very powerful piece. But 17.e5 Nh5, threatening 18...c4, is good for Black.

17...Nxf6 18.dxc5 dxe4 19.Nxe4 Nxe4 20.Qxe4 Qxc5

Black's pressure on the h8-a1 diagonal is uncontested.

21.Rd7 Rad8 22.Rhd1

If 22.Rxf7, then 22...Rxf7 23.Qxe6 Qf5.

22...Rxd7 23.Rxd7 Qg1+

Question 3: What does Black play after 24.Rd1?

24.Kd2 Qf2+ 25.Kd3 Qf1+ 26.Qe2 Qxf4 27.Qf3 Qe5 28.Qb7 a5 29.Qc6 Qxb2 30.Ke2 Qe5+ 31.Kf1 h5 32.Rc7 Qf4+ 33.Ke2 Bd4 34.Rc8 Qe3+ 35.Kd1 Bc3 36.Rxf8+ Kxf8 0-1

The Rook

Rooks should be placed on open files.

Illustrative Game 3

Alatorzeff

GM Jose Capablanca

Moscow 1935

1.d4 Nf6 2.c4 e6 3.Nc3 d5 4.Bg5 Be7 5.e3 O-O 6.cxd5 Nxd5 7.Bxe7 Qxe7 8.Nf3 Nxc3 9.bxc3 b6 10.Be2 Bb7 11.O-O c5

Black opens the c-file and will later occupy the file with his Rooks.

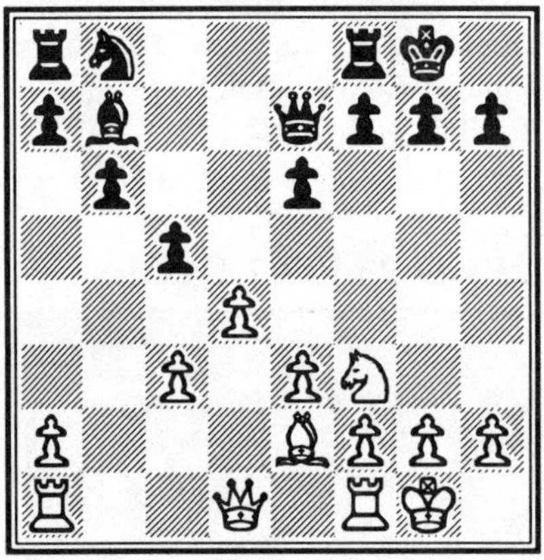

12.Ne5 Nc6 13.Nxc6 Bxc6 14.Bf3 Rac8 15.a4 cxd4 16.cxd4 g6 17.Bxc6 Rxc6 18.Qd3 Qb7 19.Rfb1 Rfc8 20.h3 a6

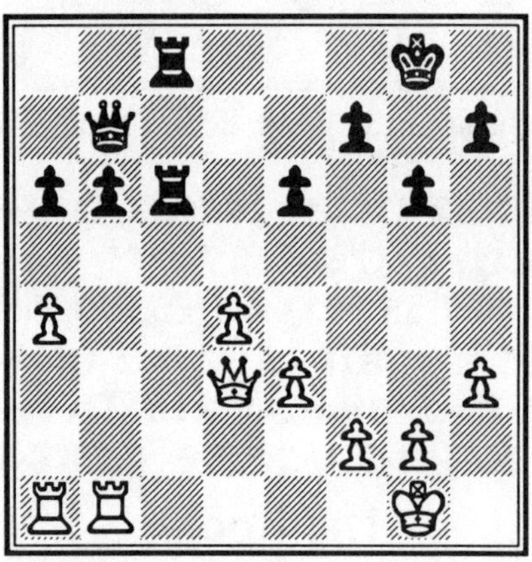

In order to meet 21.a5 with 21...b5.

21.Qa3 Rc2 22.Qd6? Rxf2!

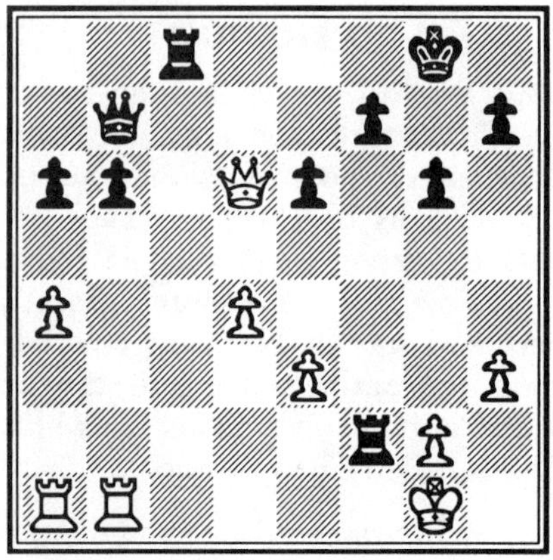

Question 4: How does Black reply to 23.Kxf2?

23.Qg3 Re2 0-1

The King

The King will usually only be activated in the endgame. In the opening it should be castled as soon as possible and should be kept tucked away in safety in the middlegame. Otherwise the King will be exposed to attack. An important rule of chess is that to tell whether an attack is going to succeed, count the number of attackers and the number of defenders. If there are more attackers than defenders, the attack will usually succeed.

Illustrative Game 4

GM Savielly Tartakower

GM Alexander Alekhine

Nottingham 1936

1.d4 Nf6 2.g3 c5 3.Nf3 d5 4.Bg2 cxd4 5.O-O Bg4 6.Nxd4 e5 7.Nf3 Nc6

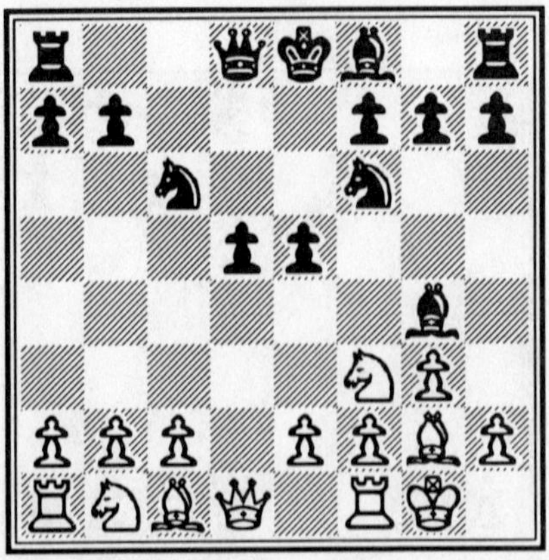

White has played the opening dubiously, as Black has been allowed to occupy the center.

8.h3 Bf5 9.c4 d4 10.Qb3 Qc7

This is bad because of White's 13th move. Better is 10...Qd7.

11.e3 Be7

Black needs to complete his development and castle as soon as possible.

12.exd4 exd4 13.Bf4 Qc8 14.Rd1 O-O 15.Nxd4 Bxh3 16.Nxc6 bxc6 17.Bxh3?

Allowing Black's Queen to get a strong attacking post. White needed to complete his development with 17.Nc3.

17...Qxh3 18.Qf3 Ng4 19.Nc3

This Knight was needed to defend the kingside. Better is 19.Nd2 followed by 20.Nf1.

19...f5!

Threatening 20...Bc5, which if played immediately would have been met by 20.Ne4.

20.Qg2 Qh5 21.Re1 Bc5 22.Nd1 g5 23.Be5 Rad8

Threatening 24...Rxd1, to which there is no defense.

24.Bc3 Rxd1 25.Raxd1 Bxf2+ 26.Kf1 Bxe1 27.Rxe1 f4

Activating the Rook.

28.gxf4

If 28.Re7, then 28...Ne3+ 29.Kg1 Qd1+ 30.Kh2 fxg3+ winning.

28...Rxf4+ 29.Kg1

Will Black's attack succeed. Yes. There are three attackers (Queen, Rook, and Knight), but only one defender (the Queen).

29...Nh2!

Question 5: What does Black do if White takes the Knight?

30.Re3 Rf1+ 31.Qxf1 Nxf1 32.Kxf1 Qf7+ 33.Kg2 Qxc4 34.Re7 Qd5+ 35.Kh3 h5 0-1

The Queen

The Queen usually plays a reserve role to the other pieces in the opening, but its strength will grow in the middlegame. *The most important rule of chess is that the pieces need to be active and coordinated.*

Illustrative Game 5

GM Alexander Alekhine
GM Jose Capablanca

St. Petursburg 1914

1.e4 e5 2.Nf3 Nc6 3.Bb5 d6 4.d4 exd4 5.Nxd4 Bd7 6.Nc3 Nf6 7.O-O Be7 8.Nf5?!

This leaves White with a weak pawn on f5.

8...Bxf5 9.exf5 O-O 10.Re1 Nd7 11.Nd5 Bf6 12.c3

In order to develop the Queen Bishop without losing the b2-pawn.

12...Nb6

Forcing White to exchange off his active d5-Knight.

13.Nxf6+ Qxf6 14.Bxc6 bxc6 15.Qf3 Rfe8 16.Be3 c5

Depriving the White Bishop of the d4-square.

17.Re2 Re5 18.Rae1

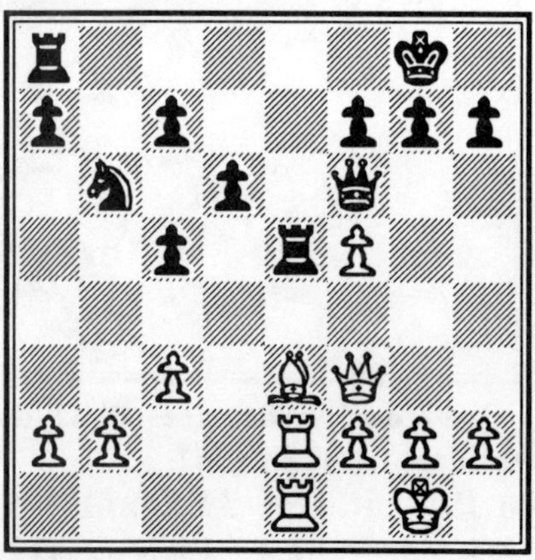

If Black tries to win back his pawn with 18...Qxf5, then much of his advantage will dissipate after 19.Qxf5 Rxf5 20.Bxc5.

Question 6: Can Black play 18...Rxf5

18...Rae8 19.Qb7

Going after Black's weak queenside pawns. But this move has a drawback.

19...Qxf5 20.Qxc7 Qe6 21.Qxa7

White has won a pawn, but there is something seriously wrong with his position. What is it?

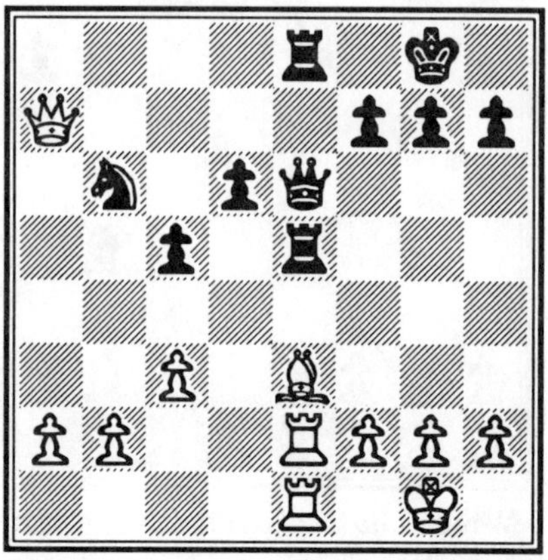

White's Queen is completely shut off on the side of the board, while Black's pieces have mobilized in the center and on the kingside. Note how beautifully Black coordinates his pieces.

21...Nd5 22.Kf1

Trying to relieve the pin on the e-file. White wants to bring his Queen back into play by Qa4 and Qc2. Therefore, Black must strike before that happens.

22...Nf4 23.Rd2 Nxg2!

The decisive blow.

24.Kxg2 Qg4+

25.Kf1

Question 7: What does Black do on 25.Kh1

25...Qh3+ 26.Ke2 Rxe3+! 27.fxe3 Qxe3+ 28.Kd1 Qxe1+ 29.Kc2 Qe4+ 30.Kb3?

30.Kc1 would have offered more resistance.

30...Qc6 31.a4 d5 32.a5 Qb5+ 33.Ka3 Rb8 34.Ka2 h6

Black wants to be able to move his Rook off the back rank.

35.a6 Qb3+ 0-1

Question 8: How does Black finish off the game after 36.Kb1?

Strategy and How to Form a Plan

After the opening is over and the middlegame is reached, the position must be evaluated. Who has the better position? Where are the weaknesses. Where should the pieces be transferred to? What diagonals and files should be controlled?

After this assessment is made, one must draw up a plan to carry out strategic operations. Usually there is not just one single plan. There are a series of little plans as the position changes or if your opponent does something unexpected, forcing you to change plans.

Here is how Yasser Seirawan evaluates a position and then forms a plan from the game Fischer–Spassky, Belgrade 1992:

1.e4 c5 2.Nc3 Nc6 3.Nge2 e5 4.Nd5 Nge7 5.Nec3 Nxd5 6.Nxd5 Be7 7.g3 d6 8.Bg2 h5 9.h4 Be6 10.d3 Bxd5 11.exd5 Nb8

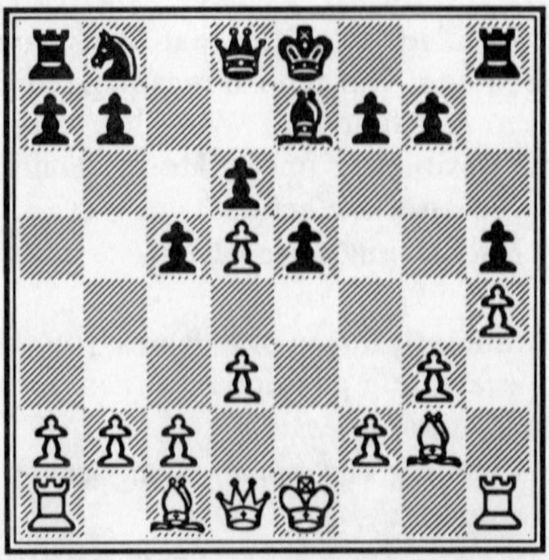

"This is an excellent position to test your strategical knowledge. How would you evaluate the position?

Let's add up the plusses and minuses. Material is equal. White has the Bishop pair. With the center blocked this advantage is nullified. The flanks appear to be in balance. Black will have to spend a tempo to play ...g7-g6 protecting the h5-pawn. That means an extra tempo for White.

Now to the plans. Black's task is easy. He needs to reposition and improve his minors. To make *his* position work, White will have to open some lines. He has three possibilities, b2-b4, d2-d4 and f2-f4. The idea of g2-g4 must be rejected because it is too weakening.

Which of the three plans is best?

Everyone knows to look in the center, so this is easy. White should play c2-c3 and d3-d4. Right? Not so fast. If 12.c3 f5 13.d4 cxd4 14.cxd4 e4, White is left with two useless d-pawns. Hmmm. The b2-b4 idea Black can meet by b7-b6 and wholesale trades on the b-file. That leaves f2-f4. But, is it so promising? Such a plan would open up the a1-h8 diagonal, making Black's Bishop powerful. Also the g4-square might become a useful outpost for

Black's Knight. Things aren't so easy for White!

On Black's side, his plan is straightforward: ...Nb8-d7, ...g7-g6 and f7-f5, ...Nd7-f6. After that Black would be better. This type of reasoning forces us to conclude that White has to open the position at once. He can't afford not to force the action."

Fischer now played 12.f4.

Similarly in you own games, you want to evaluate a position and then decide on a course of action.

Planning can occur at any stage of the game.

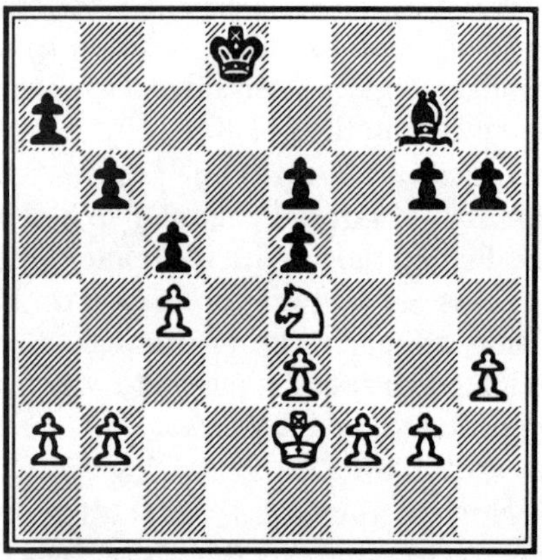

Alekhine–Euwe, London 1922 (variation)

White is much better here. Both his pawn structure and minor piece are superior. But the breakthrough will not be easy.

Here is how Alekhine formulates a plan (from *My Best Games of Chess*):

"*1st phase.*–23.h4! followed by g4 and g5 on which Black will have nothing better than ...h5, seeing that the exchange of Pawns abandons the square h4 to White's Knight.

2nd phase.–b3 followed by Kd3, Nc3 and Ke4.

3rd phase.–the manoeuvring of the White Knight to d3 after which Black must immobilize his King on d6 in order to be able to defend the doubly attacked e-pawn.

4th phase.–And lastly f4! forcing the win of the e- or the g-pawn, after which the advantage secured will be decisive."

Sometimes you form a plan by directing your forces at your opponent's weaknesses, such as an attack against the opponent's King.

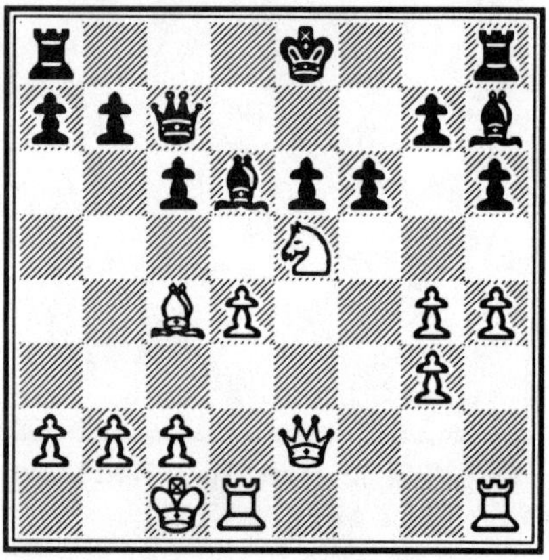

Tal–Fuster, Portoroz 1958

1.Bxe6 fxe5 2.dxe5 Be7

If 2...Bxe5, then 3.Rhe1 Bxg3 4.Bd7++ Kf8 5.Qe7+ Kg8 6.Be6#.

3.Rhf1

Threatening 4.Bf7+.

3...Rf8 4.Rxf8+ Bxf8 5.Qf3 Qe7 6.Qb3

Threatening 7.Bd7+ Qxd7 8.Rxd7 Kxd7 9.Qxb7+.

6...Rb8 7.Bd7+ Qxd7 8.Rxd7 Kxd7 9.Qf7+ Be7 10.e6+ Kd8

Or 10...Kd6 11.Qf4+.

11.Qxg7

Black loses a piece after 11...Be4 12.Qe5.

Often a plan is based on attacking a pawn weakness. Here is a very simple example of this from a King and pawn endgame:

Cohn–Rubinstein, St.Petersburg 1909

White has a serious weakness at h2. Black will tie White down to this weakness by moving his King to h3. Then he will advance his kingside pawns, forcing exchanges, then the King will go west from h3 to capture another pawn weakness:

1...Kf6 2.Kd2 Kg5 3.Ke2

A counterattack on the queenside would come too late. Work out the moves for yourself.

3...Kh4 4.Kf1 Kh3 5.Kg1 e5 6.Kh1

Or 6.e4 g5 7.Kh1 h5 8.Kg1 h4 9.Kh1 g4 10.fxg4 Kxg4 11.Kg2 h3+ followed by 12...Kf3.

6...b5 7.Kg1 f5 8.Kh1 g5 9.Kg1 h5 10.Kh1 g4 11.e4

No better is 11.fxg4 hxg4 12.Kg1 f4 13.exf4 exf4 14.Kh1 g3 15.fxg3 fxg3 16.hxg3 Kxg3 winning.

11...fxe4 12.fxe4

Or 12.fxg4 hxg4 13.Kg1 e3 14.fxe3 e4 15.Kh1 g3 winning.

12...h4 13.Kg1 g3 14.hxg3 hxg3 winning.

Before commencing with a plan, it is important to be able to evaluate a position. Based on the positions we have just seen, here are some possible questions you can ask yourself:

1. Am I ahead, behind, or even in material?
2. Are my pawns well placed and how do they compare with my opponent's?
3. How much freedom of action do my pieces have and how do they compare with my opponent's?
4. Are the King's safe or exposed to attack?
5. What is the threat?
6. What sort of pawn offensive must I aim at?
7. Is there a favorable exchange of pieces?
8. Is there any piece working only at half speed?
9. Are there any holes in my or my opponent's position?
10. Are some squares of particular importance?

The exact questions will depend on the position.

Exercise 9

From this Capablanca game reason out what advantages White has and what is the best plan.

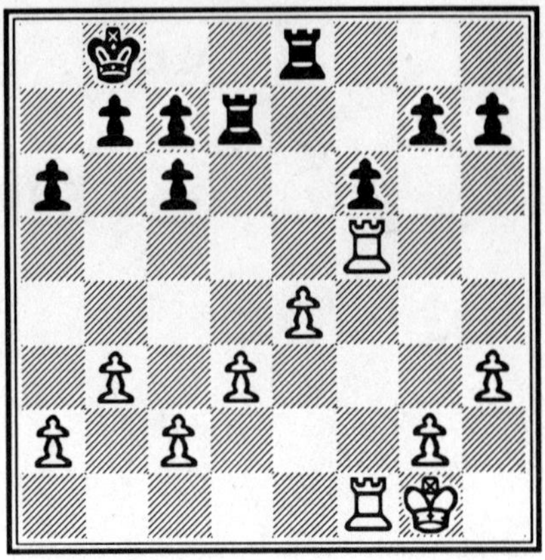

Tactics and How to Analyze

Much of the time even strong players spend on chess position involves thinking "If I go there, then he can either play this move or that move. If he plays this move, then I play there. But then he plays there. So I can't play that move..."

If you are able to efficiently analyze, then you will play a very strong game of chess. Much of this efficiency will come from having a strong intuitive feel for where the pieces should go (Rooks on open files, long diagonals for the Bishop, strong outposts for the Knight...) and an excellent positional judgement (pawn structure and weak points).

Some positions involve very little move-by-move anaysis, rather thinking based on general considerations (where to move each piece to, how to create weaknesses in the opponent's position, what points in his own position need strenthening).

Other positions are too complex for such simple judgement.

It is a good exercise to practice anayzing positions alone or with friends.

This is how Yasser Seirawan describes analyzing a position with a very strong player:

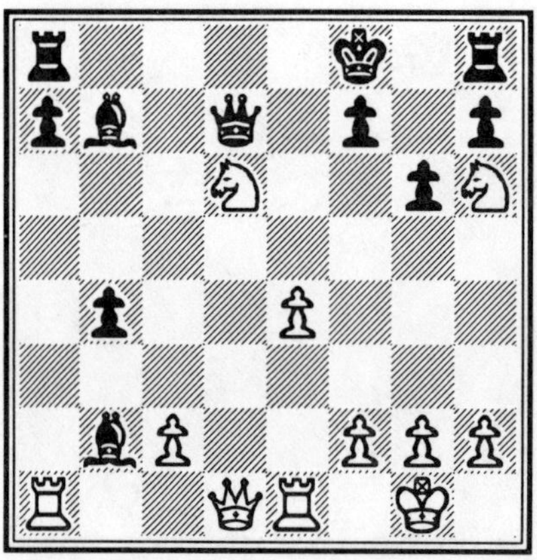

Fischer–Spassky, Sveti Stefan 1992

(*Black played 17...f6 in this position which may not be the best move.*)

"Right after the game Bobby and Boris held a postmortem and considered that the position after 17.Nxh6 was critical. Boris was sure that 17...f6 was a mistake. The players immersed themselves in the forcing sequence 17...Bxa1 (probably the best practical try) 18.Qxa1 Qxd6 19.Qxh8+ Ke7.

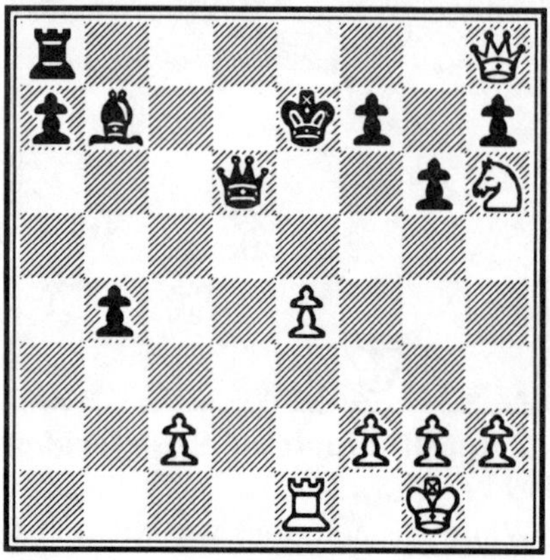

The next day Bobby, Eugenio Torre, Svetozar Gligorich, Yvette Nagel and I spent a late afternoon analyzing this position. It is an excellent position for practical work. I suggest you take a few minutes to look at the lines following 20.Qxh7 and 20.Qg7.

Initially, Bobby was strongly for 20.Qxh7, munching a pawn. He got bogged down over the line 20...Rf8 21.h4 (to clear the back rank and pound home h4-h5) 21...Qd2 22.Re3. White seems to be on a joyful attacking crunch, but his pieces are misplaced: 22...Qxc2 23.Qg7 (since 23.h5 runs into ...Qd1+xh5+) 23...Qc1+ 24.Kh2 Qc5, again restraining h4-h5. Now Black has two passers on the queenside and his King can trot to safety.

Fischer spent a lot of time trying to make 25.e5 Bd5 26.h5 work, but came away dissatisfied. At length he was talked into declining the h7-cutie. "Man, I really want that guy!" he exclaimed. We began looking at 20.e5 Rxh8 (20...Qxd2!?) 21.exd6+ Kf6 22.Re7 Bd5 before Fischer's "Nah" ended things there. Finally, 20.Qg7 Rf8 21.Ng8+ Rxg8 22.Qxg8 a5!? (White's Queen is trapped) 23.Qg7 a4, when despite being an Exchange down Black is still kicking. Indeed, the whole line isn't forced, as Black doesn't have to sac the Exchange. Bobby was vexed. "You guys are busted. Give me a sec to find the killer." Finally Bobby said, "First, give me my pawn" and produced 20.Qxh7 Rf8 21.Qg7 Qd2.

Bobby now uncorked his killer: 22.Qa1! What a shot! Suddenly, White has a crushing coordinated attack. He threatens 23.Nf5+ gxf5 24.exf5+ Kd7 25.Rd1, picking up Black's Queen. If 22...Qxh6, then 23.Qxa7 regains the piece with an easy win. A line like 22...Rc8 23.Nf5+ Ke6 (23...gxf5 24.exf5+ Kf8 25.Qh8 mate) 24.Nd4+ Ke7 (White has gotten his Knight back into the game, all with tempo.) 25.Rd1 Qc3 26.Qxa7 nets two pawns and the attack. We were forced into the ending 22...Qc3 23.Qxc3 bxc3 24.f3 a5 25.Ra1 Ra8 26.Ng4 a4 27.Kf2 a3 28.Ke3 a2 29.Kd4 Ra3 30.Ne3–this is hopeless for Black!–(Fischer). We all had to concede that Bobby is as sharp an analyst as ever."

Of course, the rest of us cannot hope to analyze a position like Bobby Fischer.

To learn to analyze better, an excellent guide is *Think Like a Grandmaster* by Alexander Kotov. Although his method is very ambitious, the recommendation made is worth its weight in gold: Pick out candidates that seem to be good moves in a particular position. This will lead to a tree with a branch for each candidate move. *In analyzing complicated variaitons one must examine each branch of the tree once and only once.* Wandering to and fro will just lose time and cause confusion.

As an excellent exercise, pick out positions that are well analyzed from a book, close the book, and write down your own analysis. After a fixed amount of time, compare your analysis with the book's.

Very importantly you want to be able to analyze accurately without making any tactical errors. Answer the following questions:

10. White can quickly end the struggle. How?

11. It's Black's move. Does he lose a Bishop?

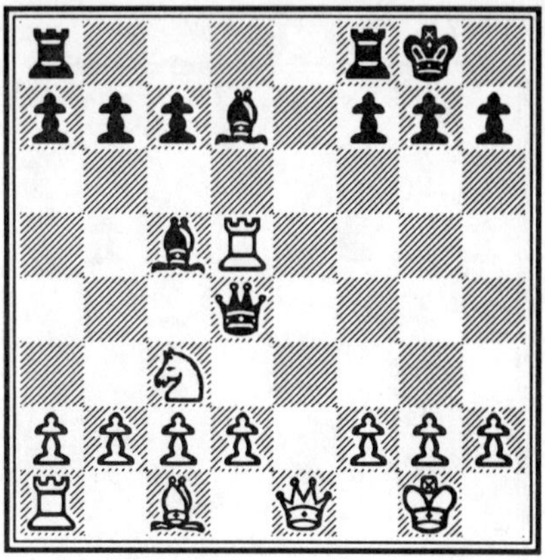

12. White's has the move and his pieces are very active. Can he take advantage of this?

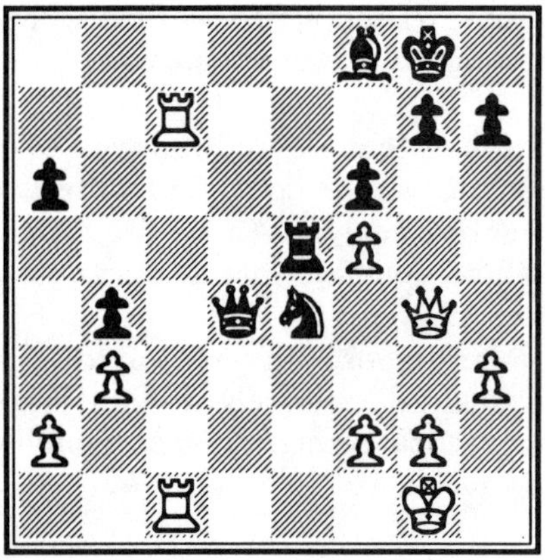

13. Can you find a way for White to breakthrough?

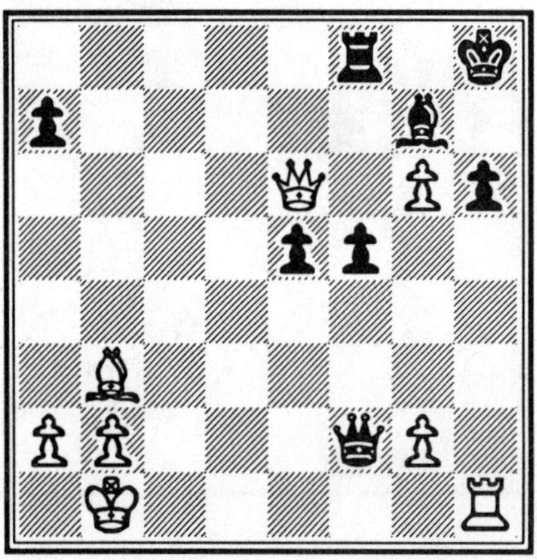

14. What move would you play for White?

15. Even in the simplest positions, the game can come to a sudden end. Can you find Black's move?

16. White has a way to break through. What is it?

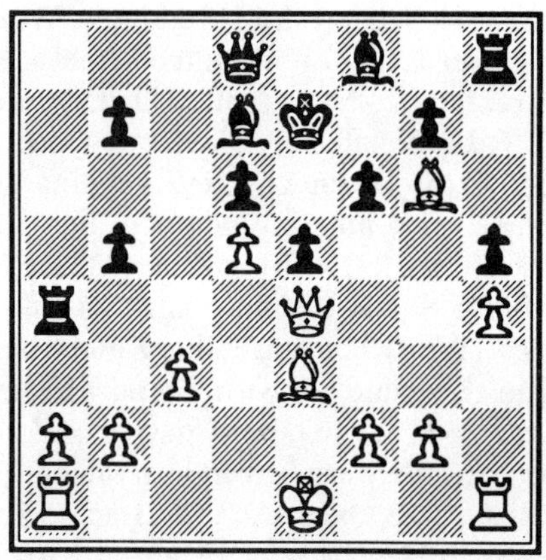

17. What is Black's brilliant idea to immediately end the game?

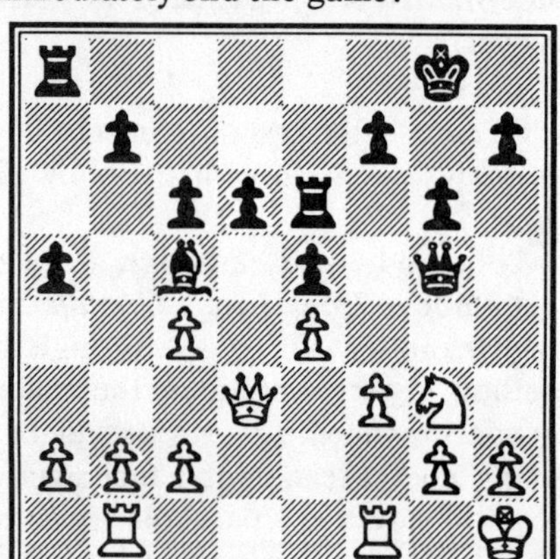

18. It's White's move. Make sure you have all the variations worked out before you do anything rash.

19. White has a strong attack. Can you find a way to force mate?

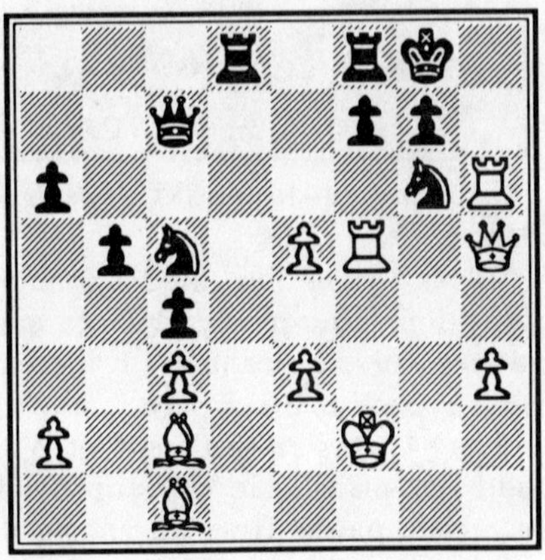

20. Black has a very powerful move. Can you find it?

21. White can nicely finish off the game. How?

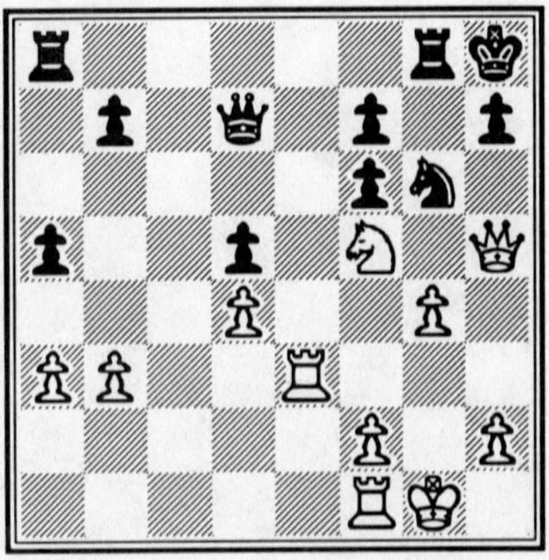

22. In this position, White played 1.Nxc8 with the idea of meeting 1...Rxc8 with 2.Qxb7. Instead, Black played 1...Rb5 and after 2.Qc2 Rxc8 remained a pawn ahead. Did White have something better on his second move?

23. White wants to force his pawns through. Is there a way?

In Summary, the reader should do the following to reach the goal of chess master:

1) Study well-annotated games played by masters. Try to understand their strategy and tactics.

2) Practice combinations as those given above.

3) Play competitively on a regular basis and annotate your games.

Solutions:

Question 1: 26...bxa4 27.Qxa4 Nb2 28.Qxa6 Ra8 wins.

Question 2: 32...Nxe3! White resigns as 33.fxe3 Bxe3+ wins.

Question 3: 24...Bxb2+.

Question 4: 23.Kxf2 Rc2+ 24.Ke1 Qxg2 25.Qb8+ Kg7 26.Qe5+ Kf8 27.Qd6+ Ke8 28.Qb8+ Ke7 29.Qa7+ Kc6.

Question 5: If 30.Qxh2, then 30...Rg4+ 31.Kh1 Rh4 wins.

Question 6: If 18...Rxf5?, then 19.Bd4 wins the Exchange.

Question 7: 25...Rg5! is decisive.

Question 8: 36...Re8 37.Rc2 Re1+ 38.Rc1 Re2 39.Qb7 Rxb2+ winning.

9. Here are Capablanca's insightful comments on the Rook ending:

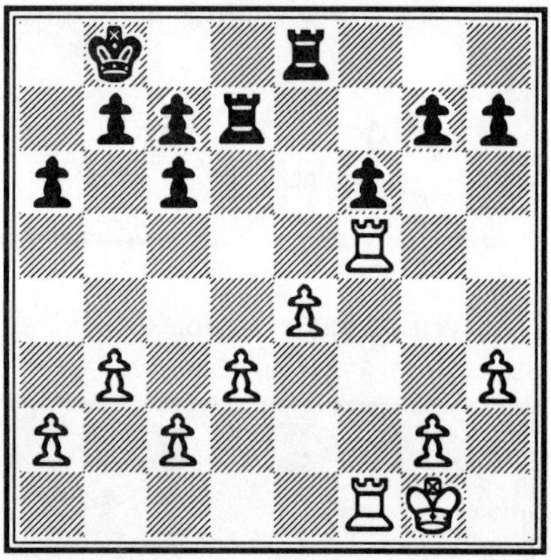

Capablanca–Janowski, New York 1913

"Black's game has the disadvantage of his doubled c-pawn, which to make matters worse he cannot advance, because as soon as Black plays ...b6 White replies b4. It is on this fact that White builds his plans. He will stop Black's queenside pawns from advancing and will then bring his own king to e3. Then in due time he will play d4 and finally e5 or g5, thus forcing an exchange of pawns on the e-file. It will be seen that this plan was carried out during the course of the game and that White obtained his winning advantage in this way. The play was based throughout on the chance of obtaining a passed pawn on the e-file, with which White expected to win."

Here is how the game continued:

1.g4

Preparing to play g4-g5.

1...b6 2.b4!

An important move, preventing

2...c5. Black should now bring his King to the kingside where the action is.

2...Kb7?! 3.Kf2 b5

Black would like to play 4...Kb6 and 5...a5, gaining counterplay on the queenside, but White prevents this with his next move.

4.a4! Rd4 5.Rb1 Re5 6.Ke3 Rd7 7.e5 Re6 8.Rbf1 Rde7 9.g5 fxg5 10.Rxg5 Rh6 11.Rg3 Rhe6 12.h4 g6 13.Rg5 h6 14.Rg4 Rg7 15.d4 Kc8 16.Rf8+ Kb7 17.e5 g5 18.Ke4 R6e7 19.hxg5 hxg5 20.Rf5 Kc8 21.R4xg5 Rh7 22.Rh5 Kd7 23.Rxh7 Rxh7 24.Rf8 Rh4+ 25.Kd3 Rh3+ 26.Kd2 c5 27.bxc5 Ra3 28.d5 1-0

10. 1.Qxf6 gxf6 2.Bh6 forces mate, Sueball-Bereben, Skopje Olympiad 1972.

11. 1...Rae8 2.Qf1 Qxf2+ 3.Rxf2 Re1#, Danielsson–Blomberg, Londsboda Junior 1967.

12. 1.Rxg7+ Bxg7 2.Rc8+ Kf7 3.Qh5+ Ke7 4.Qe8+ Kd6 5.Rd8#, Bronstein–Gligoric, Moscow 1967.

13. 1.Rxh6+ Bxh6 2.Qxe5+ Bg7 3.Qh2+ Bh6 4.Qxh6#, Wade–Kuijpers, Holland–England, Vlissingen 1972.

14. 1.Rxg6+ hxg6 2.Qh8+ Kf7 3.Qf6+ Kg8 4.Qxg6+ Bg7 5.Qxg7#, Espig–Pietzsch, Zinnowitz 1967.

15. Mihalcisin–Polajzer, Ptuj 1993. 1...Rxb2 0-1.

16. Terzic–Nurkic, Bosnia–Herzegovia 1994. 1.Qxe5+ forces mate.

17. Delekta–Geller, Cappelle la Granda 1992. 1...Qxg3! White resigns as 2.hxg3 g5 followed by 3...Rh6+ is checkmate.

18. Graudins–Karklins, Latvia 1992. 1.Rxg7! Kxg7 (if 1...Bxg7, then 2.Bxg7+ Kxg7 3.Qg5 Kh8 4.Qf6+ wins) 2.Qg5+ 1-0 as 2...Kh8 3.Qf6+ leads to mate.

19. Cudinovskih–Muravev, USSR 1990. 1.Rh8+! Nxh8 2.Qh7+ Kh7 3.Rh5+ Kg8 4.Bh7#.

20. 1.Rh8+ Nxh8 2.Qh7+ Kxh7 3.Rh5++ Kg8 4.Bh7#, Martius–Dueball, West Germany 1970

21. 1...Rd2 2.Qe3 Rgg2 wins, Toran–O'Kelly, Palma de Mallorca 1967

22.Benjamin–Yudasin, New York 1990. 2.Qa3+ wins as 2...Qxa3 3.Rd8+ mates.

23. Spassky–Milic, 1964. 1.b8=Q Bxb8+ 2.Kb7! 1-0. Black is in zugzwang.

NOTES